ADVANCED
LEARNER'S DICTIONARY
Of
COMPUTER

ADVANCED LEARNER'S DICTIONARY

Of

COMPUTER

Compiled & Edited by

A Team of Experts

ANMOL PUBLICATIONS PVT. LTD.

NEW DELHI - 110 002 (INDIA)

ANMOL PUBLICATIONS PVT. LTD.
4374/4B, Ansari Road, Daryaganj
New Delhi - 110 002

Advanced Learner's Dictionary of Computer

First Edition, 2001

ISBN 81-261-0474-0

[Responsibility for the facts stated, opinions expressed, conclusions reached and plagiarism, if any, in these volumes is entirely that of the Editor. The Publishers bear no responsibility for them whatsoever.]

PRINTED IN INDIA

Published by J.L. Kumar for Anmol Publications Pvt. Ltd., New Delhi and Printed at Arora Offset Press Laxmi Nagar, Delhi 110 092.

Preface

In the modern age computer has become the necessity of every household. No exaggeration, every walk of life has now a computer application. As such knowledge of computer is must for all.

Computer is a device, usually electronic, that processes data according to a set of instructions. The digital computer stores data in discrete units and performs arithmetical and logical operations at very high speed. The analog computer has no memory and is slower than the digital computer but has a continuous rather than a discrete input. The hybrid computer combines some of the advantages of digital and analog computers.

Planned and designed by a team of experts in the field, this dictionary is primarily meant for the students and teachers as well as computer professionals at advanced level. All the entries are judiciously selected and explained in straightforward manner. Suitable diagrams are also given to clear the idea.

We are grateful to all learned scientists whose definitions and explanations are borrowed or substantially made use of in this Dictionary.

It is hoped that the students, teachers, and the general users will find this endeavour unique, informative and useful. For making the dictionary more comprehensive and informative, constructive criticism from the readers are welcome.

—Editors

A

ABEND: *(ab-end,* n) A computer crash (from "abnormal end" error message).

Ablative Pit: An indentation (pit) burnt into the surface of CD-ROM and WORM drives as a means of recording digital information.

Above Board: In an IBM or IBM compatible PC, a printed circuit board that contains additional RAM.

Absolute Address: This is a method of assigning an address to each location in computer memory, these usually relate to some fixed, designated part of RAM or ROM and are therefore referred to as absolute addresses, they are not dependant on the present location.

abstract syntax: A syntax (set of rules for properly formed commands) not limited to a single application or platform.

access: (n) 1. A connection to the Internet; 2. A type of Internet connection (network access, dialup access, etc.); 3. The ability to perform certain activities or read privileged information.

Access Control List (ACL): A site's table of services and hosts authorized to use those services.

access privileges: Authorization for a specific level of access.

access provider: An institution providing Internet access, such as a commercial service provider, university, or employer.

Access Time: The time taken from first request for data to that data appearing on the data bus. Access time to disk or is tape is largely determined by file size and the hardware device, whether or not the read/write head has to be repositioned and whether the data file occupies a favourable sequence of disk sectors, tape sections etc. Typical hard disk access times are in the 30-80ms range.

Accumulator: A register which is used to store the results of intermediate or final calculations.

ACK: (rhymes with *pack)* 1. Acknowledgment from a computer that a packet of data has been received and verified; 2. The mnemonic for ASCII 6.

ACM: Association for Computing Machinery.

active star: A network design (a way of arranging the devices themselves in a network) in which a central hub retransmits all network traffic.

ADA: This is a high level language developed for the US Department of Defense during the 1970s. ADA is a structured language and was named after Augusta Ada, a 19th Century mathematician.

Addicted to Noise: A music magazine, featuring sound clips, on the Web at http:// www.addict.com/ATN/.

Add/Strip: A Macintosh shareware program that inserts or deletes carriage returns (ASCII 13) at the end of each line of a text file, for conversion between Macintosh and UNIX systems.

Address Bus: A set of wires or printed circuit tracks that is used for specifying addresses within the computer and its peripherals.

address command: A UUCP extension that provides additional routing and confirmation options to the basic filecopying transaction that underlies UUCP.

Address Mapping: Table (AMT) A table used to resolve physical addresses into logical addresses.

address mask: The portion of an IP address that identifies the network and subnet.

address resolution: Conversion of a physical address into a logical address.

Address Resolution Protocol (ARP): A TCP/IP protocol for converting physical addresses to logical addresses.

ADJ: (rhymes with *badge)* [Boolean operator] *Adjacent to.* A text search with ADJ between two words matches only documents in which those words are adjacent.

Administrative Domain (AD): The portion of a network overseen by a single administrator.

administrator: Someone who maintains the addresses and handles the administrative chores for a mailing list or other Internet discussion group.

administrivia: Information regarding the administration of a mailing list or moderated newsgroup, such as the announcement of a new moderator, posted to the list or group.

Advanced Program-to-Program Communications (APPC): An IBM peer-to-peer network protocol.

Advanced Research Projects Agency (ARPA): A U.S. Department of Defense agency that, along with universities and research facilities, created ARPAnet, the precursor of the Internet.

agent: 1. The process in client/server communication that handles negotiation between the client and the server; 2. A Simple Network Management Protocol program that monitors network traffic; 3. A program that performs some action on the behalf of a user without the direct oversight of the user.

AIR NFS: A Windows version of NFS (Network File System).

ALGOL: Acronym for ALGO-rithmic Language, a high level programming language developed, during the mid-1960s. ALGOL is a structured language and is regarded as a forerunner of other structured languages such as PASCAL.

Algorithm: A set of instructions that provide a solution to a given problem. Named after AI Khwarizmi, an Arab mathematician of the ninth century, author of many treatises on mathematics and algebra.

Alphanumeric: Any characters of the alphabet and the arabic numbers 0-9. This definition of alphanumeric is used to specify data types in a database.

Alpha Test: Initial testing of a new product, usually performed inhouse by the hardware-software developer.

alt A hierarchy of newsgroups in the Usenet mold but outside of Usenet proper, devoted to "alternative" topics. It is easier to create alt. groups than to create standard Usenet groups, and it's effectively impossible to remove them.

ALT Key: On IBM and IBM compatible PCs, a key that in combination with other keys invokes a particular action.

alternative newsgroup hierarchy: 1. Any hierarchy of newsgroups in the Usenet mold but not, strictly speaking, part of Usenet; 2. The alt. hierarchy in particular.

alt.fan group: A newsgroup devoted to a realworld or Net celebrity or villain.

ALU: Abbreviation for Arithmetic Logic Unit. This is part of the Central Processing Unit (CPU) and is involved in arithmetic operations, for example, A=B*(C+D/E) and logic calculations, for example, is X greater than Y.

American National Standards Institute (ANSI): U.S. organisation that develops and promotes voluntary standards in a wide range of academic and research fields.

Amiga: A personal computer produced by Commodore, based on the Motorola 68000 microprocessor.

ampersand (&): In HTML (Web) documents, used with special codes to indicate special characters (the HTML code for an ampersand itself is *&amp)*

Amplitude: A measure of the waveform of a transmitted signal. The amplitude of a sine wave is measured from the highest point of the signal to the lowest.

Amplitude modulation: A transmission technique which uses changes in the amplitude of the signal to transmit information (voice, music or data).

Analog: (adj) Representing values as physical states and changes in values as changes in physical states. In a stereo, for example, a CD player converts the digital information encoded on the CD into an analog signal sent to the amplifier.

Analog Computer: A computer designed to respond to an infinite number of variations in signal, compared to a digital computer which responds to discrete off and on (binary 0 and 1) signals, Examples of analog computer usage include monitoring temperature, voltage and current readings in a power station. Each of these parameters can attain an infinite number of values, not just simply off and on. In many cases however, it is comparatively simple to convert analog signals to a coded binary signal, enabling digital computers to perform many tasks that were previously the domain of analog computers.

Analog Transmission: A method of transmitting data or information that uses an infinitely variable signal. Whereas digital transmission can only transmit off and on signals (binary 0 and 1), analog can transmit any designated value. Using photography as an example, in digital transmission it would be possible to transmit a black and white photograph, but only black and only white would be transmitted, whereas analog could transmit every possible shade of grey.

Anarchie *(anarchy)*: A Macintosh program that combines the functions of archie and FTP.

AND Gate: A logic gate that has two or more inputs and one output. It is used to detect when two or more inputs are present. Two or more inputs must read 1 before the gate makes an output.

an AND GATE

Input		Out put
0	0	0
0	1	0
1	0	0
1	1	1

Andrew File System (AFS): a set of network protocols that makes remote files accessible as if they were local (as contrasted with being available via. FTP).

angle brackets: They surround return addresses in e-mail headers. In IRC channels, MUDs, and some e-mail and Usenet posts, angle brackets surround descriptions of actions or expressions: for example, <looking over my left shoulder> or <groan>. Similarly, some use <grin> or <g>.

Animation: Movement of graphics objects during a computer program.

annoybot: (n) An IRC bot that pesters real users.

anonymous FTP: The most common use of FTP, the Internet file transfer protocol. FTP sites that allow anonymous FTP don't require a password for access—you only have to log in as *anonymous* your e-mail address as a password.

anonymous remailer: A service that provides anonymity to users on the Net who wish to send mail and Usenet posts without their actual e-mail address and real name attached. Instead of sending mail or posting articles directly, users send them to the anonymous remailer, with special header lines indicating the ultimate destination and the pen name of the user.

ANSI: Abbreviation for American National Standards Institute, a powerful industry association of the USA. ANSI is active in negotiating and promoting industry standards, many of which have been adapted into international standards by CCITT and/or ISO. ANSI standards exist for many aspects of computer usage, for example programming language such as ANSI C and the ANSI defined Data Dictionary.

answers Moderated: Usenet news groups dedicated to the posting of FAQs (frequently asked questions) and their answers.

Any key: Some programs prompt you to continue by telling you to press any key. This means that any key you press will suffice to continue the process. There is no specific "Any" key.

AOL: The standard abbreviation for America Online, from aol.com, the subdomain and domain for that online service.

API: *(ay-pee-eye) Application* Programming Interface.

Apple: A personal computer, first produced in 1976, which is based on a Motorola micro-processor. Apple Corporation, the manufacturer of Apple Computers, was founded by Steve Jobs and Steve Wozniak, originally working out of a suburban garage.

AppleTalk: Apple Computer protocol for data transmission/network connections.

application: A computer program that performs a specific function for the user, as contrasted on one hand with a document and on the other with a shell, environment, or operating system.

application layer: The top (seventh) layer of the OSI Model.

Application Programming Interface (API): Software that controls communication between a program and a computer environment.

April Fool's jokes: Beware strange news or e-mail posted on April Ist.

Arc: A DOS file extension that indicates a compressed archive file.

Archie A client/server application that gives users access to databases that keep track of the contents of anonymous FTP *archives*—hence the name.

Archie client: The archie program you run to get information from an archie server.

Archie for Nextstep: An archie client for the Nextstep operating system.

Archie server: The archie program that houses a database listing the contents of anonymous FIT sites, in a searchable form, accessible to archie clients.

Archie site: A computer with an archie server running on it.

Archive: 1) A secure storage area for disks and tapes. Many organisations archive their data off-site for security reasons (mainly fire risk). 2) An operating system or software application feature that allows data to be compressed into a disk/tape space saving format for archiving.

Archive file: A file that has been compressed or that contains a number of related files.

Archive site: 1. An FTP site, a computer on the Internet that stores files; 2. Any repository of information accessible via the Net.

Are you on the Net? This question usually means, "Do you have an e-mail address that can be reached from the Internet?"

Argument: A value that is passed to a program module each time the module is called by the main program. The use of arguments allows a module to perform programming tasks on similar, but not necessarily identical datasets.

ARMM: Dick Depew's Usenet robot (ARMM stood for *Automated Retroactive Minimal Moderation* inten-ded to retroactively cancel anonymous posts and post follow-ups, it spun out of control instantly during its first run on March 31, 1993, posting,follow-ups to its own follow-ups, spamming several newsgroups, and crashing systems all over the Net.

Article: A Usenet newsgroup post, that is, a message posted publicly and available for reading by every subscriber to the newsgroup(s) it's been posted to.

Artificial Intelligence (AI): A field of computer science research aimed at understanding how the human mind thinks and creating intelligent machines that can learn from their experiences.

Asbestos: Usenet or e-mail posters expecting flames often speak of donning asbestos overalls or other protective gear.

ASCII (*askee*): American standard *code* for informa-tion interchange. ASCII is a standard character set that's been adopted by most computer systems around the world.

ASCIIbetical order: A sorting order based on the ASCII character set that corresponds to English alphabetical order but sorts symbols and numbers before letters and uppercase letters before lowercase letters.

ASCII file: A file containing text only. ASCII files are easier and quicker to transfer than binary files.

ASCII file transfer: A method of file transfer by which an ASCII file is sent as a sequence of characters instead of as a sequence of binary data

(1s and 0s). When necessary, newline characters are changed by the filetransfer program.

ASCII font: A "font" created out of plain ASCII characters, usually found in sig blocks, often spelling out the writer's name.

ASCII graphic: A drawing composed of ASCII characters, such as an enormous medieval sword, an attempt to limn Bart Simpson, or a map of Australia.

aspect ratio: The proportion of height to width. Most computer displays have a 3 to 4 aspect ratio.

assigned numbers: Standard numbers for ports, sockets, and so on, established by the Internet Assigned Numbers Authority.

Association for Computing Machinery (ACM): An association of computer researchers and developers that serves as both a source of technical information and an umbrella group for numerous SIGs.

Asynchronous: (adj) Not happening at the same time. The word is used both for data transmission and for human communication.

Asynchronous transmission: A transmission method that uses start bits and stop bits to regulate the flow of data, as attachment opposed to synchronous transmission, which uses a clock signal.

AT commando: *(ay-tee commands)* Hayescompatible modem commands, most of which begin with AT (for "attention"), such as *ATZ*, which resets a modem's factory initialization (the basic settings for the modem when it was created).

atob: *(ay-to-bee)* A UNIX program that converts ASCII files to binary files.

attribute: (n) A setting associated with a file that indicates whether the file is a *system file* (a protected file created by the operating system and not to be tampered with), a hid*den file* (one that won't show up in normal file listings), or an *archive file* and who can read it.

Autonomous System (AS): A set of routers overseen by a common administrator, using the same protocol.

A/UX: Apple's UNIX clone for the Macintosh.

B

Backbone cabal: A nowdefunct group of largesite administrators who set in place most of the procedures for Usenet newsgroup creation and orchestrated the Great Renaming of the Usenet hierarchy.

Back door: A security loophole that a programmer to evade restrictions and enter an otherwise secure system. If a back door remains after the software is released, it becomes a security risk.

Background: This term is used to describe tasks that are handled by the CPU during normally "idle" time. For example, printing a document while the user continues with another task. Background tasks are supposedly "user transparent", that is, the user is unaware of their progress.

Backslash: The \ character, often found above the Enter key on keyboards. In DOS paths, it separates directories and subdirectories; in UNIX, it precedes switches (commandline arguments).

Backspace:(v) To use the Backspace key to move a cursor to the left and in the process delete characters on a computer screen.

Backspace key: A key found directly above the Enter key on most computer keyboards, often used to erase characters to the left of the cursor.

Use of the Backspace key in terminal emulations that don't support it sometimes leaves the original text onscreen, followed by one H character for every time Backspace is pressed. This results in the digital equivalent of an unzipped fly.

Backup: The process of making a copy of a file for archive purposes. For example, files from a hard disk directory may be copied to floppy disk for safe keeping. Backups ensure that data files 'and/or software can be recovered in the event of major equipment problems or a disaster, such as fire or flood. It is normal business practice to keep backup copies in a separate building. Many large organisations contract archival storage of their backup tapes/disks to security companies. Backup copies may or may not be working copies of the original file. Some backup procedures use data compression to reduce the amount of tape or disk space required for each file. In this case it is necessary to run a restoration program before the data can be accessed by the software application.

Bad Sector(s): Those sectors on a floppy/hard disk identified by the operating system as having physical and/or electrical problems. Bad sectors are not included in the File Allocation Table and are not used for data storage.

Bad Thing: Something generally or widely accepted to be bad. Racism is a Bad Thing. So is spamming Usenet.

Balanced line: A cable containing electrically equal wires such as a twistedpair cable.

Balun: *(bal-un, n)* An impedance-matching device that connects a balanced line (containing electrically equal wires), such as a twisted-pair cable, to an unbalanced line (containing electrically unequal wires), such as a coaxial cable.

Band Printer: A line printer that has its character set embedded on a metal band. The band is moved horizontally at high speed whilst a series of hammers make contact with the band, transferring the image onto the paper. Characters are printed seemingly at random across the paper, the printer detects when a particular character is at the right position at the right time, and words are not necessarily printed consecutively from left to right.

Bandwidth: The difference between the lowest and highest frequencies of a transmission medium. A telephone circuit has a very small bandwidth, whereas a microwave channel has a very wide bandwidth. Bandwidth is a measure of the amount of information (voice, data, video) that a particular communication medium can carry.

If you post a uuencoded binary file containing a 9xl2 24-bit image to a talk newsgroup, you're definitely wasting bandwidth. But even if you have a sig block of over four lines, if you include too much quoted text in your follow-up post, or if you continue a flame war, you too may be accused of wasting bandwidth.

Bandwidth hog: A user or process that consumes more than his, her, or its fair share of bandwidth.

Bang: (n) An exclamation point. It precedes each site in a UUCP mail path. In some UNIX programs, it enables the user to shell out.

Bang path: A UUCP mail path that specifies every site along the way from the sender to the receiver. Although it is rarely necessary any longer to specify the route your mail will take (there are many interchangeable routes on the Internet), mail headers still sometimes include the entire bang path back to the sender.

Bar: A popular dummy variable used by programmers in place of specific terms, such as the dummy mail address foo@ bar.baz.

Bar Chart: A type of chart (graph), that uses horizontal or vertical bars to indicate the relative values of several data items.

Bar Code: A series of thick and thin black lines printed on many consumer products so that they can be identified by check-out machines. A unique bar code is assigned to each product by a national bar code association. Bar codes are sometimes referred to as Universal Product Codes.

Barfic: (n) An ugly ASCII graphic.

Barney: 1. A dummy variable used by programmers in examples in combination with fred; 2. A large, purple, talking dinosaur who is praised and excoriated in various Usenet newsgroups.

Bart Simpson: A popular subject of ASCII graphics in big, ugly sig blocks.

Baseband: (adj) Signal transmission that uses the entire bandwidth of the medium, the method used by most LANs.

BASIC: A high level programming language originally developed by John Kemeny and Thomas Kurtz. The name BASIC is an acronym for Beginners All-purpose Symbolic Instruction Code. BASIC was designed to introduce beginners to computer programming techniques. It has since outgrown this purpose and, in its many proprietary forms, is a very powerful language with high productivity.

BASICA Proprietary (IBM) version of the programming language BASIC.

Basic Encoding Rules (BER): A technique for encoding data (preparing data for transmission) defined in ASN.1 (Abstract Syntax Notation One).

Basic Rate Interface (BRI): An ISDN (Integrated Services Digital Network) service that connects LANs (local area networks) via 64 kps data channels.

Batch: (adj) 1. Noninteractive, handed without interaction, as *in batch mode;* 2. All at once, or in a bunch, as in *batch printing.*

Batch File: A collection of commands that are grouped together under one file name. When the file is run the commands are executed to provide the desired result. Batch files are frequently used to cut down on the number of keystrokes required to achieve a particular task.

Batch Processing: A method of processing data en masse rather than as individual transactions. Batch processing is used extensively in mainframe computer applications, for example, generating pay slips once a month, updating stock control records once a week etc. Batch processing is also known as offline processing, since it is not interactive with an external information source.

baud: *(bawd)* Usually confused with bits per second (bps), baud is technically the number of times per second that your modem changes the signal it sends through the phone lines.

Baud Rate: This is used in communications to indicate the number of times that a signal changes per second. Typical rates are from 300 9600 Baud. High Baud rates indicate fast data transmission.

Baz: A popular dummy variable used by programmers in examples in place of specific terms, such as the dummy mail address foo@bar.baz.

B-board: A BBS. Newbies often refer to, Usenet newsgroups as bboards.

BBS A *bulletin board system,* communications software that runs on a PC a enables users to log in via modem, check messages, communicate in topic groups, engage in real time chats, and (sometimes) access the Internet.

Bcc: *Blind carbon copy.* Borrowed from the world of paper memos, the blind carbon copy list is a list of additional recipients of an e-mail message whose names and addresses will not appear in the header.

Beam: (v) 1. To transfer a file to someone (from *Star Trek* and other science fiction); 2. To wish someone well via e-mail. (n) An expression of support sent electronically.

Beige toaster: A derogatory term for a Macintosh.

Benchmark Test: A test used to evaluate the performance of hardware and/or software, using a set of industry standards and reference marks as the basis for evaluation. Most countries have a standards institute or an association of recognised testing authorities and laboratories.

Berkeley Internet Name Domain (BIND): UNIX name server software developed and distributed by the University of California at Berkeley.

Berkeley Software Distribution (BSD): A version of UNIX developed and distributed by the University of California at Berkeley.

Bernoulli Box: A secondary storage device which uses removable disks. The technology of a Bernoulli Box differs slightly from a hard disk in that it uses the "Bernoulli Effect" to keep the read/write head clear of the data surface. A typical Bernoulli Box has a capacity of 40MB, with an access time of about 20ms. Named after Daniel Bernoulli, a Swiss scientist who investigated many properties of fluid dynamics. See also Hard Disk, Removable Disk Pack.

Beta:*(bayta)* Prerelease software made available to a small group of testers (often called *beta testers)* in the "real world" to put it through its paces and identify any bugs or design flaws that did not show up when it was tested by the developers before being shipped commercially.

Beta Test: The final part of product testing. In Beta testing the product is handed over to individuals or corporate users for "real-life" evaluation. Feedback to the manufacturer/developer from the Beta test group is then used to fine tune the product before release to the general public.

Bezier Curve: A graphics format used to describe part of a graphics outline or parts of the outline of a font. Some printer command languages use Bezier Curves to define outlines and shapes. Named after Pierre Bezier, a French automotive technician who first used Bezier Curves to define shapes on the bodywork of Renault cars.

B1FF: Also called B1FF. A prototypical newbie on Usenet, looking for k00l warez. kool is B1FF-speak for cool, warez-pronounced *wares,* from software-means pirated game software). He posts in all caps, substitutes numbers for letters, uses exclamation marks liberally, and has a huge sig block-all of which are marks of a BBS culture of the 1980s populated mainly by teenage boys.

Bigendian: (adj) 1. A storage format in which the most significant byte has the lowest address, as opposed to littleendian; 2. The way Internet addresses arc written in the United Kingdom starting with domain, then subdomain then site (the opposite of the standard order on the rest of the Internet).

Bigot: Someone who believes beyond all rational discussion that one particular type of computer is the best (or the worst),

Big red switch: Sometimes abbreviated BRS, the on/off switch on a computer or any crucial toggle switch that when switched off, will shut clown the system.

Big seven: The seven toplevel Usenet hierarchies (also known as traditional newsgroup *hierarchies): comp., misc..* news., rec., sci., soc., and talk.

Bin 1) A tray on a printer for holding blank paper or preprinted forms. A bin may also be used for receiving the finished work. 2) A miscellaneous directory on a hard disk, often used as a location, for operating system and service programs.

Binaries newsgroup: A Usenet newsgroup dedicated to the posting of uuencoded binary files, often .gif or .jpg image files. Some sites won't carry binaries newsgroups because their uuencoded binaries consume so much bandwidth (and storage space on the news site computers).

Binary: 1. Base 2, a numerical system using two digits: 0 and 1 (compare with *decimal-base* 10, a numerical system using 10 digits: 0 through 9); 2. A binary file.

Binary Coded Decimal: Digital computers all use some form of binary numbers for their internal operations, however humans use decimal numbering, and there is a constant need for conversion from one system to another. This conversion can be long and complicated, hence a method of encoding which is a mix of decimal and binary systems has evolved. This is known as Binary Coded Decimal.

Each digit is converted to its binary equivalent as follows,

874 becomes 1000 0111 0100

The BCD then represents each digit of a decimal number by a 4-bit binary number. Only the 4-bit binary numbers from OM to 1001 (0-9) are required. BCD does not use the numbers 1010, 1011, 1100, 1101, 1110 and 1111, in fact only 10 of the 16 possible combinations are used. This six unused combinations are referred to a "forbidden codes" BCD arithmetic needs to take the forbidden codes into consideration and scrub them as, and when they occur.

A BCD number is not the same as the binary number. A straight binary code takes a complete decimal and represents it in binary format. BCD converts each decimal digit individually as shown by the number 137 in binary and format,

137 = 10001001 in binary

137 =0001 0011 0111 in BCD

BCD takes 12 bits to represent 137, whereas binary code requires only 8 bits. For a given number BCD requires more bits than for the equivalent binary. The main advantage of BCD, however, is in the relative ease of converting to and frorn decimal numbering. This ease of conversion is especially important from a hardware/software point of view.

Binary data: Computer information stored in the form of O and Is (most program files and image files, as well as some documents, are stored as binary data).

Binary File: A file that is stored in a condensed binary format. These are usually non-text files. Programs (executable files) are typically stored as binary files.

Binary Synchronous Control (Bisync): An IBM protocol for controlling communictions in synchronous environments.

Binary file transfer: A file transfer in which every bit of the file is copied exactly as is (as opposed to a text is transferred to whatever format the receiving machine prefers).

Binary Numbering: A numbering system whose largest digit is 1. Therefore when counting in binary a given digit will progress from 0 to 1 and then recycle back to 0. Computer memory (ROM, RAM) uses electronic and electromagnetic components which can exist in only one of two states (off or on) and which can be switched very rapidly from one state to another. As there are only two possible states for each memory locality (off or on) the information (data) stored in a computer uses binary notation, with the binary digits 0 and 1 corresponding to the two possible states of a particular memory location.

A single binary digit is called a bit (a 0 or a 1). Bits are usually organised into a continuous sequence of eight bits and are then referred to as a byte. The number of bytes is then called the word length. Different computers have different word lengths, however modern machines have a word length which is usually a multiple of eight bits, typically 8, 16 or 32 bits. Since eight bits make a byte, a 32-bit word represents lour bytes of data.

Binding: The linking of the main body of a program to its modules, library routines etc.

BinHex: A Macintosh program that converts binary files to ASCII files so that they may be transmitted via-e-mail

BIOS: Abbreviation for Basic Input Output System, the hardware and software used to provide the fundamental input/output capablilities of a computer. The software is generally embedded into ROM as firmware. BIOS functions can be called from many programming languages.

BIOSIS/FS: A database of biological and biomedical research available through OCLC.

Birds of a Feather (BOF): An ad hoc discussion group on a conference program.

Bis In modem standards, an enhancement to the standard, but not a completely new standard. V.32bis is an improvement on V.32, for example.

Bisymchronous: (adj) Communication in which the sending and receiving takes place at the same time.

Bit: A binary digit, the smallest unit of computer information, transmitted as a single on or off pulse symbolized by 1 or 0.

Bit bucket: 1. An imaginary place where extra bits land when they "fall off a register" the computer equivalent of forgetting to "carry the 1" during addition, 2. The computer equivalent of the circular file, or the place where all lost socks and pencils go.

Bitnet: A hierarchy in the Usenet mold populated by newsgroups gated to BITNET listserv mailing lists.

Bit: A short form for binary digit. A bit is capable of recording "off" or "on" conditions, usually represented by the digits 0 (off) and 1 (on). A group of eight binary digits is referred to as a byte, whereas a large run of bits is referred to as a bitstream.

Bit Mapping: The use of groups of bits (dots) to create an alphabetic character or a graphics image.

Bitmap Font: A font created by the use of bit mapping, generally these cannot be scaled or rotated.

BITNET: *Because Its* Time *Network, a* huge network distinct from the Internet but fully connected to it, used largely for e-mail and listserv mailing lists.

Bits per second (bps): A measurement of the speed of a medium, meaning the number of bits that can pass through the medium in one second.

Bit Rate: A method of measuring data transmission speed.

Bits Per Second: The rate of data transmission measured in number of bits per second. Bits per second (abbreviation bps) is sometimes used interchangeably with Baud Rate, however the two measures of transmission speed are not necessarily equal. A local area network is likely to operate at 19200bps, whereas a low speed modem may operate at 300bps.

Bitstream: 1) A proprietary design of typefaces (soft fonts). 2) A sequence of bits transmitted on the data bus or over a data communications line.

Bitty box: A derogatory term for a personal computer, from the workstation or mainframe point of view.

Biz: A hierarchy in the Usenet mold dedicated to commercial and business communication. Advertising is explicitly permitted in the biz. hierarchy.

Black hole: The place where missing e-mail messages or Usenet posts are said to have disappeared to.

Bleed: A term used in desktop publishing and commercial printing, which refers to an illustration running of the edge of the page.

Block: (n) A standard unit of data the size varies from system to, system) measured in terms of storage or transmission.

Blocking Factor: On a computer tape records may be grouped together (blocked) so as to allow faster access (tape transport) times. The block is selected first and then the block. The number of data records in a block is referred to as the blocking factor Typical blocking factors are from 820.

Boolean Variable: A program variable that can have only two values, true or false. Named after George Boole, a 19th century mathematician. The following PASCAL code demonstrates the use of a boolean variable,

```
PROCEDURE FILDAT (VAR FN : STR20; VAR NOENTRY: BOO-
LEAN);
BEGIN;
REPEAT
FN := " ;
NOENTRY := TRUE; (*Boolean variable NOENTRY is assigned the
value "TRUE"*)
GOTOXY (25,5);
WRITE ('DATABASE FILE NAME _');
READLN (FN);
IF LENGTH(FN) > 8 THEN          BEGIN
    GOTOXY(18,7);
    WRITE(^G,'File name too long - Press Enter to Continue ');
    READLN(DUM);
    NOENTRY:= TRUE;
    END
ELSE NOENTRY : = "FALSE";
UNTIL NOENTRY; (*loop is repeated until NOENTRY = "FALSE"*)
END;
```

Bogometer: *(boe-gom-i-ter)* A mythical device that measures bogosity or bogon flux.

Bogon: *(boe-gon)* A mythical basic particle of bogosity,

Bogon filter: A mythical device that can limit the flow of bogons.

Bogon flux: A mythical measurement of the strength of a field of bogons.

Bogosity: (boe-goss-i-ty) The extent to which something is bogus

Bogus: (adj) 1. Lame, stupid, false, useless; 2. Fake.

Bogus newsgroup: Silly or joke-named Usenet-style news-groups created by pranksters with the necessary access privileges.

Boink: (n) A party at which participants of a Usenet newsgroup meet in the flesh.

Bomb: (v) To crash, to suffer from an unrecoverable error.

Bookmark: In gopher clients and Web browsers, a reference to a menu or page to which you might want to return later, In gopher clients, bookmarks appear together on a gopher menu.

Boolean search: A method of searching a database or text in which Boolean operators are used to limit and specify the search criterion.

Boot: An initiating routine that is read into RAM when a computer is first turned on. This provides the necessary environment for subsequent loading of A or part of the operating system, software applications and data. The boot is in effect a part of the operating system. The verb "to boot" is often used to indicate the process turning on a computer. Booting a computer is jargon for turning it on.

Under MS-DOS the files IO.SYS and DOS.SYS are first loaded and then the file CONGIG.SYS is read.

The contents of this file setup or modify the operating environment. The file COMMAND.COM is then loaded and this initiates a search for, and execution of, the file AUTOEXEC.BAT. Some of this routine may be altered by programmers, for example, a specific copy of COMMAND.COM can be loaded, but the basic routine is still the same. Once the boot process is over the computer is ready for use.

Boot Disk: In disk operating systems the boot routine, also called the boot record, is stored on disk. A computer that uses a disk operating system cannot be used without first having access to the boot record. 'Me boot disk, containing the boot record, may be a floppy disk or a particular part of a hard disk.

Boot Record 1) Part of the operating system that provides the bare essentials to get a computer up-and-running.

Boot Record 2) The area of secondary storage where the boot information is stored. This is usually in a low address level, for example, sector 0 of a hard disk.

Boot Sector: The area of secondary storage where the boot information is stored. This is usually in a low address level, for example, sector 0 of a hard disk.

Bootstrap Loader: The first part of a boot record.

Bootstrap Protocol (BOOTP): A protocol for booting diskless nodes on a network.

Boot Tape: Many computers store the boot routine on tape, usually a cassette. A computer that uses a tape operating system cannot be used without first having access to the tape drive containing the boot tape.

Border Gateway Protocol (BGP): An exterior gateway protocol based on the External Gateway Protocol used by NSFnet,

'bot: A robotic entity on the Net that automatically performs some function that people usually do. Many IRC channels are kept open by semipermanent 'bots that stay connected just as real users might. In the past, people have spammed Usenet by employing 'bots to automatically post (robopost) reams of redundant text.

Bounce: (v) E-mail that fails to reach its destination and returns to the sender is said to have bounced.

Bounce message: A message from a mailer daemon indicating that it cannot find the recipient of an e-mail message and is returning it to the sender.

Bozo filter: A kill file. It allows you to filter out the bozos whose Usenet posts you don't wish to, see.

Brain dump: (n) An undifferentiated mass of information, often in response to a simple question (by analogy from core dump, screen dump, etc.).

Branch: (n) 1. An intermediate part of a logical tree, somewhere between the root and a leaf, 2. A participant in a tape tree who receives copies of a tape from her parent and makes copies for her children (who may themselves be branches or leaves).

Bridge: A device that connects two net work components (such as zones) that use same protocols.

Brief: (adj) An operating mode for some systems and applications in which the prompts and reports of activities are abbreviated or skipped altogether.

Broadband: (adj) Signal transmission that can carry multiple signals at once, each on separate channels, each taking up a portion of the bandwidth.

Broadcast: (n) A transmission sent to all hosts or clients at once, such as "System going down in 10 minutes. Please finish up".

Broadcast storm: The confusion and possible network breakdown that occurs when a faulty packet is broadcast, generating multiple incorrect packets in response, ad infinitu.

Break Point: A command in a program that stalls the execution of the next command, pending the programmers input and/or perusal of program variables. Often used to help debug a program.

Break Signal: A special character or set of characters used to terminate a data communications session or to stop program or batch file execution.

Broadband Transmission: A transmission method which divides the transmission medium into a number of channels, each of which can carry data circuits. Broadband circuits typically have a bandwidth of four megahertz or greater.

Brouter: *(brow-ter)* A device that combines the functions of a bridge and a router, controlling transmission from one network component to, another (as a bridge) and from the network to the Internet (as a router).

Brownout: A significant drop in mains power supply to a lower than normal level. Brownouts are usually caused by electricity demand overloads and means that the number of Hz (cycles per second) drops below the normal 50Hz. A brownout may not necessarily affect computer operation.

Browse: To skim an information resource on the Net, such as Usenet, gopher-space, or the Web.

Btoa: *(bee-to-ay)* A UNIX program that converts binary files to ASCII files.

BUAF: (bee-you-ay- eff) *Big, ugly ASCII front* Character sets made from ASCII characters, often generated by special programs and often used to spell out names in sig blocks.

BUAG: *(bee-you-ay-gee) Big, ugly ASCII* graphic. Large, often crude drawing composed of ASCII characters, such as a map of Australia, a medieval sword, the U.S.S. *Enterprise* etc., often appearing in a sig block.

Bubble Memory: A form of static memory which uses impregnated garnet as the storage medium.

Bubble Sort: A programming algorithm that is used to sort data into alphabetic or numeric order. The lowest value data are said to "bubble" to the surface.

Buffer: A temporary storage location for data used by many software applications to improve file handling capabilities. Buffers are also used where there was a vast difference in processing capability between one device and another. For example, the CPU may send data at very high speed to a printer but because the printer is an electromechanical device cannot turn this data into printed output at the same rate. A buffer provides a temporary storage location for data, enabling the CPU to quickly unload its data and proceed to a more important task.

Bug: (n) A flaw in a program (from the expression "working the bugs out"). Also, jokingly defined as an undocumented feature.

Bugg: (adj) Said of software, unstable, unreliable, full of bugs.

Bulletin Board Service: A commercial data communications network where users (subscribers) can send messages, get advice on software, upload, download programs etc.

Bundle: A term used to describe a computer and associated peripherals and software that is sold as a package.

Bundled Software: Software that is sold with a computer system.

Bunyip: The company formed by the people who invented archie.

Bureau: An organisation that provides data processing services to another organisation.

Burst Errors: In data communications this is a series of errors that occur in close proximity (in a burst). In practice most errors occur in bursts.

Bursting: The process of separating continuous form paper into separate sheets.

Bus: Pronounced "buss" or "buz", this is a set of wires or printed circuitry used for transmission of data or power(data bus, power bus). It is also used for addressing particular parts of memory (address bus) and for control functions (control bus). Typically, buses use 8, 16 or 32 parallel wires, enabling 8, 16 or 32 bits of information to be transmitted in parallel to one another. A 32-bit bus provides many times the processing capability of an 8-bit system, however the full potential of a larger bus is not always realised as, for example, 16-bit processors are sometimes used with 32-bit buses.

Business Infornation Processing: A generic term used to describe the processing of data and transactions in a business environment. Examples include, generating invoices or travel reservations such as airline tickets, cancelling a cheque, producing a payroll output.

Bus topology: *Also daisy chain* a network architecture in which all nodes are connected to a single cable.

Buzz word: Also stop word, a.word so common that it is useless to search for it (such as and, *address, record,* and so on). Most searchable databases have lists of buzz words and filter them out during searches.

By hand: (adv) Executed step-by-step by a human being, instead of automatically by a computer process.

Byte: This is a unit of data storage that is roughly synonymous with one character of data storage. A byte is eights bits (binary digits) of information. On most computers a byte is the smallest amount of memory that can be reached via the address bus.

Cache: A special area of primary memory set aside to be used as a temporary store for programs, parts of programs or data. Cache is pronounced cashay or caysh, from the French word cachier-to hide. Cache memory is usually quite small (typically 64KB on a PC that may have 4MB of RAM and 80MB of hard disk storage) and has very high access speeds. It is used to raise the overall processing speed of a computer. Information that will be required frequently or within the next few instruction cycles are loaded into cache memory for subsequent access by the CPU. Since the required information is in cache memory and not on hard disk or floppy disk, the access time is much reduced. Because of its high access speed, cache memory is expensive and requires special control circuitry.

Cache Controller: Electronic circuitry that controls' read/ write operations to cache memory. The controller may be a chip or discrete components.

Call for Votes: (CFV) A stage in the Usenet newsgroup creation process, after the Request for Discussion (RFD).

Camera-Ready Artwork: Printed material that is ready for photographing at commercial printing premises. Once photographed the camera-ready artwork image is then used to make the printing plates.

Campus-Wide Information Server (CWIS): The information system for a college or university, usually including schedules, announcements, job listings, bulletin boards, calendars, and so on.

Cancel: On Usenet, to delete an article after you've posted it. It takes a while for the article to vanish everywhere, as the cancel message has to catch up with the propagating article.

Canonical: Deriving from an official source. In Star Trek newsgroups, facts that come from any of the television series or movies is considered canonical; 2. Prototypical, to programers.

Canned Program: A commercial software package that is available for sale to the public or ready for use by a particular organisation.

Caps Lock Key: A key on a computer keyboard that provides access to upper case letters (a-z becomes A-Z) but not the "second function" of any other key. Compare this to the Shift Key which affects alphabetic characters and the "second function" of other keys.

Capture: (v) To save text as it scrolls across the screen. Captured text can be read white offline.

Card: A printed circuit board, added to a computer to enable it to control an additional device.

Card Reader: An electromechanical device that reads data from a sequence of paper cards. The cards have a series of preperforated tabs which can be removed to form a pattern recognisable by the card reader. The card reader converts each pattern into machine code for use by the processor. Card readers are infrequently used today as the cards are prone to user error, easily destroyed and generally not reusable.

Caret: The ^character. Indicates an exponent (for example, x^2 means x^2, that is, x *squared).*

The caret is also used in e-mail and Usenet posts to underscore and emphasize text on the preceding line, as shown in the example at the top of the page.

Careware: A form of shareware in which the creator of the software requests that payment be made to a charity.

Carpetbagger: Someone who comes to the Internet looking to, make a quick profit in what they consider to be a ripe, undeveloped territory (borrowed from the American Reconstruction period's pejorative term for Northerners looking to make a quick buck off the wartorn South).

Carriage return: A character that moves the cursor back to the beginning of a line (ASCII 13), usually starting a new line in combination with a line feed character.

Carrier: A signal constantly transmitted by a modem over a phone line as a reference for the modem on the other end of the line.

Carrier Signal: In data communications, a signal established on the transmission medium for modulation by data signals.

Carrier detect: The notice that a modem has identified the carrier signal from another modem over a phone connection.

Carrier Sense Multiple Access (CSMA): A protocol that enables multiple devices to transmit on the same channel, by "listening" for the sounds of other devices and only transmitting when the line is clear.

Carder Sense Multiple Access with Collision Avoidance (CSMA/CA): A version of CSMA in which devices can detect impending collisions and avoid them.

Carrier Sense Multiple Access with Collision Detection (CSMA/CD): A version of CSMA in which devices can detect collisions as they occur and resend the corrupted signal.

Cartridge Tape: This is a magnetic tape, about 8mm wide, which is housed in a plastic cover approximately 12cm x 12cm. Cartridges are used mostly on mainframe computers, and provide compact data storage (sequential access) and easy loading. They are often used as a back-up system and typically offer up to 2000MB storage. Cartridge tapes used on personal computers have capacities in the 60-100MB range.

Cascade: A series of one-line follow-up posts, each a play on the previous one. Each post contains all of the previous ones leading up to the latest change, usually in ever-shortening lines, due to the rows of >'s (or sometimes other characters) automatically inserted by newsreader positing commands to indicate an inclusion from a previous post.

Case-insensitive: Not distinguishing between upper and lowercase characters. In a case-insensitive search, *Internet, internet,* and INTERNET all match the same key word.

The DOS and Macintosh operating system are case-insensitive, as are e-mail addresses UNIX, on the other hand, is case-sensitive.

Case-sensitive: Distinguishing between upper and lowercase characters. To a case-sensitive program, *Peter,* PETER, *peter,* and *PeTeR* all mean different things.

UNIX is case-sensitive; DOS and Macintoshes are not. E-mail addresses are not case-sensitive.

Cassette Tape: A magnetic tape housed in a plastic cover, used mostly on early personal computers and on some mainframe computers to store boot information. Cassette tapes used on computers are, in general, audio cassettes.

Cat: A UNIX command (short for *catenate* from *concatenate)* that can pour the contents of one file into another or dump the contents onto the screen.

Catch up: When reading news, to mark all the articles in a newsgroup as read, to clean the slate.

Cathode Ray Tube: The technical name for the screen of a computer monitor. This name originated through the use of "cathode rays" (electron beams) in the monitor. Cathode rays strike phosphor beads on the monitor screen, thereby producing the appropriate image. Usually abbreviated to CRT.

cc: A list of additional recipients for an e-mail message in the header of the message (from carbon copy, a carrier from office-memo shorthand).

CCITT: Abbreviation for Consultative Committee on International Telegraphy and Telephony. This is an international standards organisation based in Paris, and is a member of the International Telecommunications Union. CCITT negotiates international standards for many aspects of communications.

cd: A UNIX and DOS command meaning *change directory*.

CD-ROM: Abbreviation for Compact Disk-Read Only Memory, this is secondary storage that uses optical (laser) techniques to read\write data. CDROM has a reasonably fast access time and vast storage capability. Compare this to hard disk access times and storage capability.

Cell: A data entry point on a spreadsheet. A cell occurs at the intersection of every row and column.

Cell-switching: A variation on X.25 packet-switching protocol in which data is bundled into equalsized cells.

Cello: An integrated Web browser and general Internet tool (gopher, WAIS, Usenet, mail) for Windows. Available by anonymous FTP from ftp.law. cornell.edu.

Censorship: The public spaces of the Internet (such as Usenet newsgroups, IRC, and so on) are largely free from censorship and can be noisy and childish at times. Online services, however, take more responsibility for the contents of their networks and may therefore place some restrictions on what can be written in public or even in private.

Centred Text: Text that is centred within the text block. A technique often used with headings.

Central processing unit (CPU): The heart of a computer, the part that does the "thinking."

CERN European Particle Physics Laboratory: *(surfnet)* (The acronym CERN comes from an earlier French title of the Lab: *Conseil Europeen pour la Recherche Nucleaire)* The creators of the World Wide Web and the first (text-based) Web browser, www. You can reach CERN on the Web at http://www. cern.ch/.

CERT: Computer Emergency Response Team.

Chain Printer: A line printer that has its character set embedded on a metal chain. The chain is moved horizontally at high speed whilst a series of hammers make contact with the band, transferring the image onto the paper. Characters are printed seemingly at random across the paper, the printer detects when a particular character is at the right position at the right time, and words are not necessarily printed consecutively from left to right.

Chameleon NFS: Socket, TCP/IP, and Internet tools software for Windows, made by NetManage.

Chameleon Sampler: A free collection of socket, TCP/IP, and Internet tools available via FTP from ftp.netmanage. com, in the pub/demos/ sampler directory, in a self-extracting archive file called sampler.exe.

Channel: (n) 1. The path along which one device sends a signal to another, meaning a physical cable or wire or an assigned frequency of a physical channel; 2. An IRC topic area.

Channel hopping: On IRC, jumping around from channel (definition 2) to channel.

Channel op: A privileged user of an IRC channel, able to kick antisocial participants.

Character: Any alphanumeric (A-z, a-z, 0-9), facet of syntax (! ? ' " etc), mathematical operator (= + * /) or graphics symbol. Characters are represented in computer memory by a series of bits.

Character Generator: Software embedded in ROM that will generate characters on-screen (using pixels) or on a print medium.

Character-based: Said of a computer, operating system, environment, or terminal emulation, displaying screens composed entirely of characters (as opposed to graphical images) and accepting input only in the form of characters (as opposed to mouse clicks).

Character-based interface: A computer front end which displays only characters on the screen—no graphics, no icons, no mouse pointer, etc. Many dial-up Internet connections are to UNIX boxes with character-based interfaces.

Character length: A terminal emulation setting that determines the number of bits in a character (usually seven or eight). ASCII characters require seven bits per byte (one byte per character); binary transfers may require eight bits per character.

Character string: A string of characters that must be handled as text, not as numeric data.

Character Sets: Combinations of characters grouped together by software and hardware engineers for specific purposes. For example, the "Roman" character set would contain all the characters necessary to generate a text file in any of the latin languages. A "mathematical" character set would contain all of the symbols necessary for intricate mathematical formulae and calculus. Not all characters are supported by all computer software and hardware.

Characters Per Second: A measure of printer, scanner or typist speed, usually abbreviated to cps.

Charter: The founding document of a Usenet newsgroup, it defines what constitutes ontopic and offtopic discussion, and establishes whether the newsgroup is moderated or not.

Chat: (n) 1. Synchronous (happening in real time, like a phone conversation, unlike an e-mail exchange), line-by-line communication with another user over a network; 2. The chat program itself, now largely superseded by the IRC program.

Cheapernet: Slang for the "thin" Ethernet specification, generally used in offices.

Checksum: An error-checking method in which the sending and receiving modems both sum up the bytes in a data packet and compare the totals.

chmod: *(see-aitch-mode)* The UNIX command for changing the read-write permissions of a file (from *change mode).*

Choad: (n) Slang for penis, popularized by the denizens of alt.tasteless.

Church of the SubGenius: A half-serious antireligion founded by the Rev. Ivan Stang and blending the principles of Discordianism with '50s advertising clipart images and mindnumbing homilies. SubGenii can be found in the Usenet newsgroup alt.slack and elsewhere on the Net, often talking about the deity Bob.

CIA World Factbook: A source of basic information on every country in the world, reachable by WAIS at world-factbook.src; also, one of the books made available for free by Project Gutenberg.

Cipher: (n) A code that involves character-for-character substitution (as contrasted with word-for-word substitution or other schemes), a simple example of which is rot13.

Circuit: A channel carrying an electrical current between two devices.

Circuit board: A computer card holding printed circuits.

Circuit-switched network: A network arrangement in which each node is connected to the next via a dedicated line.

Circular Reference: On a spreadsheet this is a formula embedded in a cell that uses its own address as part of the formula. For example the formula in cell AK36 might read =sum(AK15:AK36). This formula will soon produce a very large number as it Is constantly adding itself to itself.

Clari: The Usenetstyle news-group hierarchy dedicated to ClariNet news items.

ClariNet: An online news service analogous to newspaper wire services. If your service provider gets a ClariNet newsfeed, then the news is part of your overhead cost. Otherwise, you can get ClariNet news by direct subscription.

CLASS: Cooperative Library Agency for Systems and Services.

Clear channel: A 64 kps channel with its entire bandwidth available for transmission.

Clearinghouse for Networked Information Discovery and Retrieval (CNIDR): An organization supporting research and cooperation relating to information resources on the Internet (such as WAIS, gopher, archie, and the Web) and ways to search and retrieve information from them. They distribute free-WAIS, a free version of WAIS. CNIDR can be reached on the Web at http://cnidr.org/welcome.html.

Client: An application or computer that communicates with and requests information from a server. In conventional networking, client usually refers to a computer; for Internet client/server applications, client usually refers to a program.

Client/server: 1. A method of distributing information or files in which a central server application archives (stores) the files and makes them available to requests from client applications; 2. A LAN architecture, in which files and other resources are kept on a central server computer and individuals interact with the network through client computers.

Client/server application: A network application that functions with a central server as a repository of information and clients that communicate with the server arid request information on behalf of individual users.

Clip Art: A graphics file, often provided as part of a graphics software application, that includes many items of computer generated artwork. The user can select a piece of clip for later use.

Clipboard: Part of a software application that allows the user to make notes, often unrelated, whilst using another package. Clipboards usually produce ASCII text files and can store graphics files.

Clipper Chip: A U.S. government sponsored encryption standard that telecommunications industries will be encouraged to adopt when it becomes final, according to pending proposals. The Clipper Chip includes a back door that would allow government agencies to eavesdrop on communication encrypted with the chip The government would need a court order use the decryption keys, otherwise kept in escrow.) Opponent of the Clipper Chip are suspicious government following its own rules and believe that any individual or company should have access to the best encryption technology available, not just government approved encryption.

Clock: 1) The internal timing function of the CPU. High clock speeds are usually synonymous with high processing capability. Clock speeds are measured in megahertz (millions of cycles per second). The symbol MHz is also used, for example, an Intel 80386 microprocessor may easily attain speeds of 25MHz. Whilst clock speed gives an indication of processing speed there are other factors involved in completing a task quickly. These include hardware considerations and the use of memory management techniques.

Clock speeds have been rising steadily and many computer professionals wonder if there is a limit to be reached, and whether any further increases will be meaningless in the majority of applications. 2) The timing device found in many computers, providing time and date on demand via the operating system. Most use a small battery to keep running when power is removed from the computer. The clock is often located on a small circuit board or directly on the motherboard. Utility software provides a means of updating the clock, either for times or dates.

Clone: A copy of an item of hardware or software. IBM compatible PCs are often referred to as "clones".

Close: A command used by many software applications to exit from the application and/or to make sure that all open files are closed. Failure to properly close a file may result in lost or corrupted data.

Close: (v) To hang up a telnet, FTP, or other remote connection.

Clueless newbie: A derogatory term for a beginner who POSTS IN ALL CAPS or betrays some ignorance of the Net. We were all clueless newbies once.

Cluster: The smallest amount of disk space that can be allocated by an operating system for data storage, cluster sizes are typically about 1KB. The actual size is set down during formatting and is related to the capacity of the disk.

Coalition for Networked Information (CNI): A coalition of libraries and research organizations dedicated to the sharing of information over computer networks.

Coax: (co-ax) Slang for coaxial cable.

Coaxial Cable: A type of cable whose conductors share a common axis. Coaxial cables have excellent transmission qualities and are widely used for linking the nodes of a Local Area Network.

CODASYL: Acronym for Conference on Data Systems standardisation of data systems.

Code: Any sequence of bits or Characters that is used to represent a group of characters (words), commands or series of instructions.

Coding: The process of writing a program. A program is said to contain so many "lines of code".

Cognitive dissident: The vocation, coined by Electronic Frontier Foundation cofounder John Barlow, for those who challenge the status quo in cyberspace.

Coke machine: At one time or another, there have been many soda machines on the Internet. This usually means that some device monitors the machine, keeping track of how many cans of soda are in each slot and possibly how long they've been there (i.e., how cold they are). This device then updates an information file that can usually be fingered from anywhere on the Internet.

Cold boot: (v) To start a computer that's completely off.

Collating: The process of sorting computer output (hard copy) into a logical sequence for human usage. In the case of a publication this would be in, page number order. Depending on the hardware used, hard copy output may be produced in reverse order or in the case of multiple copies, all of the page 1s maybe printed first, followed by all of the page 2s etc. In either case it is necessary for someone to collate the output. Most up-market printers will collate automatically, provided that they are instructed to do so.

Collision: What happens two devices try to use the same channel at the same time.

Colon: In URLs, a colon (:) appears after the protocol name., In e-mail and Usenet posts, colon sometimes indicate included text.

Colorado Alliance of Research Libraries (CARL): An alliance of seven libraries that contribute to a database containing abstracts of thousands of journals.

Column: 1) The vertical grouping of text, as in a newspaper. Most word processors and desktop publishing packages allow text to be aligned in columns. 2) In a spreadsheet, columns are the vertical groupings of cells, typically columns are designated by alphabetic characters whereas the horizontal groupings (rows) are given numerical characters. 3) On a printer, a measure of the maximum paper width. Using a 12 point font, the maximum number of columns on an A4 (290x17Omm) sheet in portrait mode is about 80. The number of columns alters with different fonts sizes. Using an eight point font, the maximum number of columns is about 240 on A3 paper (landscape mode).

.com: The Internet domain dedicated to commercial entities, generally in the United states.

COMDEX: An annual exposition of computer dealers, held in the USA every year. The name COMDEX is derived from COMputer Dealers EXposition.

Comm: Communications (sometimes spelled com), usually in the context of communications software, a communica-tions port on a computer, and so on.

Comma: In Usenet newsreaders, you can often crosspost your article to several newsgroups simply by listing them one after another, separated by commas(,). Likewise, in most mail programs, you may list several e-mail recipients the same way, separated by commas.

Command: An instruction given to the CPU either by a software application, for example, a database package initiating the creation of a new file, or directly by the computer operator via the operating system. For example, on a VAX machine the command DIR lists the currently available files. In either case the command will be converted to machine code and acted upon by the CPU.

Command Driven: An operating system or software application that responds to direct typed commands from the computer user. The alternative is a menu driven system in which the computer operator passively selects an item from a menu. Some applications combine both direct commands and menus. Menu systems are popular as, in many cases, they reduce the amount of typing and thinking involved in using a computer.

Command Language: This is a language used for communicating with an operating system, hardware device or software application.

Command line: A single line of text, with a Prompt, often at the bottom of the screen, where the user may enter commands directly. DOS and UNIX are command-line operating systems; Macin-tosh, Windows, and X Window are graphical environments that do not automatically make a command-line available.

Command-line interface: A front end that allows or forces the user to memorize and type commands at a prompt, as opposed to one that allows or forces the user to click graphical elements and select commands from pull-down menus.

Command mode: A program mode in which you can enter commands. In vi, the UNIX text editor, users start off in command mode and will be frustrated if they try to start typing text. First, they must switch to insert mode.

Command Processor: A generic command file used to recognise some of the rudimentary commands of an operating system. The MS-DOS generic command processor is COMMAND.COM. Programmers often substitute this file with one of their own creation.

Comment: A brief lire of commentary embedded into a computer program. Comments aim to provide a "roadmap" through a program, enabling programmers, including the original writer, to follow the overall logic of the program. Since comments occupy a line of code it is best to be brief, rather than verbose in commentary.

Other languages use different characters to indicate comments. In FORTRAN comments are preceded by the character C, in PASCAL comments may be enclosedbetween brackets { comment } or brackets and asterisks (* comment *), and in C between slashes and asterisks, / * comment */.

Commercial access provider: A service provider that charges for access to the Internet, as opposed to employers, universities, and free-nets, which provide access for free.

Commercial Internet Exchange (CIE or CIX): An organization of service providers that represents the interest in making commercial transactions acceptable and secure over the Internet.

Common Carrier: A commercial organisation or government authority that provides communications facilities for the business community and government. In Australia, Telecom Australia and OTC are common carriers. Common carriers are an essential part of data communications as they enable smaller organisations to gain access to otherwise prohibitively expensive data communications hardware. Common carriers, through their size, are also able to support large scale capital expenditure and to employ a large pool of technical expertise.

CMMU: Abbreviation for Cache Memory Management Unit.

Communications program: A program that operates a modem and provides terminal emulation so that the user can log in to and communicate with a remote computer.

Communications Terminal Protocol (CTERM): Part of DECnet's virtual terminal service (protocols that allow a user to emulate a different terminal type) specifications.

CMOS: Abbreviation for Complementary Metal Oxide Semiconductor, a particular type of integrated circuit technology that provides low power consumption.

Comp: A Usenet hierarchy devoted to computers.

Compact Pro: A Macintosh shareware compression program. Files compressed with Compact Pro have a.*cpt* extension.

Compatible: Used to describe the relationship between different hardware devices and/or software applications. An ABCD Computer may be "compatible" with an WXYZ Computer, or database software Q-Base may be compatible with Z-Base.

Compiler: A part of the operating system or programming environment that reads instructions from: source code, typically a high-level language such as FORTRAN or PASCAL, and translates this source code into an object file. A compiler usually "compiles" the whole program, from first to last line, before attempting to link and run the program.

Compiler Directive: Instruction(s) written into a program (source code) which direct the compiler to perform a particular task. These are commands rather than programming code to be converted into machine code.

Compile-Time: The time during which source code is compiled into an object file. This may include linking the main body of a program to its modules, library routines etc. An error occurring during the compilation process is called a compiletime error.

Compile-Time Error: An error that occurs during compilation of source code.

COM port: The communications port on a computer. On PCs, it's a serial port.

Compress: (v) The squish a file in order to save disk storage space.

Compression: A method of squishing a file in order to save disk storage space or the amount of squishing.

Compu$erve (CI$): A mildly derogatory name for CompuServe that refers to its expensive connect time fees.

CompuServe Information Manager (CIM): A program that provides a graphical interface (or front end) for CompuServe, available for both Macintosh and Windows.

Computer Aided Design: The use of a computer and specialised software to generate two and three dimensional drawings. Given that images on a computer screen can be changed and manipulated much more easily than those on paper, the use of CAD techniques is a major breakthrough in design processes.

Computer Aided Instruction: The use of a computer as a training tool. Many interactive programs have been developed for this purpose. CAI provides a comfortable training environment where each participant (trainee) can pace themselves and take time out to check references, or to repeat particular sections of the training program. Abbreviation CAI.

Computer Aided Manufacturing: The use of a computer and specialised software to assist in many manufacturing processes, not only the physical processes involved but also in planning, scheduling, tooling etc.

Computer Aided Software Engineering: The use of a software package to assist in the design and coding of further software.

Computer Architecture: The way in which a computer is configured in terms of disk drives, primary memory, data connections etc. It does not, in general, refer to the physical attributes of the computer.

Computer Crime: Used to describe any crime that involves illegal entry (physical or otherwise) into a computer or its data storage. Computer crimes are typically theft, destruction or manipulation of data for personal gain.

Computer Emergency Response Team (CERT): A network-security task force available round-the-clock to assist Internet users with security problems.

Computer Floor: A false floor that is typically 2530cm above the actual floor level. Computer floors allow the cabling at a computer site to be conveniently and safely located out of the way, providing a clutter-free work environment.

Computer geek: Someone who enjoys messing around with a computer, not necessarily as a programmer or at the same level of sophistication as a hacker. This is riot necessarily a derogatory term. It depends on the context and the company.

Computer Literacy: This refers to the ability of a person to cope with a computer based working environment.

Computer-mediated communication: Any form of communication aided and abetted by computers, including, but not limited to, e-mail, chat, and conferencing.

Computer Network Technology: The communications techniques covered so far have been concerned with centralised systems. Terminal networks are all built around a central computer; similarly remote job entry stations are usually connected to a single computer. In the remaining chapters some of the problems and techniques of a network of intercommunicating devices are discussed. The devices at present connected to networks are usually generalpurpose computers, with their own terminal networks. One reason for networking multiaccess computers, rather than terminals or smaller devices, is that these computer systems already existed when networking was proposed. A second reason is that the protocols used in computer networks are very complex so that only a large computer system would have sufficient spare computing power to implement them. However, terminals can be directly attached to a network, by using a dedicated computer. In the near future computer networks will become as widespread as the telephone network, and large scale integration will enable cheap processors to handle the protocols. The result will be the networking of every sort of computing device. The current trends indicate that powerful, single user, workstations will replace terminals for network use. The workstations will be directly connected to a local area network and use the resources of larger computers via the network.

This chapter is primarily concerned with the technology used to connect the computers and devices that make up a computer network. For the purposes of description the range of technology has been divided into three areas

1. wide area networks
2. Radio and satellite broadcast networks
3. Local networks

The network technology includes the techniques used to interconnect the computing devices and physically transfer information from one computing device to another.

Wide area networks: The term 'wide area network' is applied to a network that covers a large physical area, say a whole country or large area under one administration. Such an area may be worldwide where a multinational organisation owns the network. The basic communication media used are dedicated circuits, usually of about 50 kHz bandwidth.

Where digital circuits are available the bandwidth would be 64K bps. The recent introduction of fibre optics in longdistance trunks has make link bandwidth of 2-3M bps available. Wide area networks will be using these links over the next few years. Examples of such networks are PSS, ARPANET, Tymnet, Telenet, etc.; details of some of these networks are given at the end of this section. For reasons explained in chapter 3, the physical circuits are usually provided by a PTT, although in the case of PSS the whole network is also run by the PTT.

Although 50 kHz bandwidth seems to be a lot compared with the 3 kHz nominal bandwidth of the voice telephone line, it is not very much when highspeed or large-volume transfers of information are required. Even at these high speeds the channel capacity is a resource that needs to be used efficiently.

It is now necessary to see how information can be transferred from one computer to any other on the network. The problem falls into two parts. The first is that of transferring information via a medium, such as a wire. The second part is concerned with addressing and routing. If there were only two computers on a network, then they could be connected by two channels, one for each direction, and whatever one computer transmitted the other would be bound to receive. When more computers are added, the bidirectional connection.

Fully connected network: Solution can be extended by having each computer connected to every other computer by a full duplex connection. To send a message to a particular computer the appropriate connection is selected; thus the routing of a message is carried out by the sender. Using a dedicated connection between every computer on the network is very expensive. If there are n computers on the network then $n(n-1)/2$ lines are needed, and have to be paid for! As a single computer would not normally be communicating with every other computer on the network at the same time, most of the lines would be unused in a fully connected network. Therefore to increase the utilisation of the connection circuits, their number is reduced, and switching is introduced within the network.

There are three forms of switching that can be used in communications: circuit switching, message switching, and packet switching.

Circuit switching: Circuit switching is used on the PSTN to connect telephone subscribers. To use it for a computer network each computer would have a private circuit to a local exchange, and the exchanges would be connected to form a network.

Whenever two computers wish to exchange information, a physical path is established between them via the exchanges. The path is then disconnected when the connection is closed. The circuit has been ,switched' by the exchanges. This method of connection is not used on established computer networks. The major disadvantages of circuit switching are

1. The cost of the equipment is very high, whereas the resulting circuit is not necessarily of high enough quality for computer communications.
2. The resulting circuit can only be used by the two computers on the call, thus the equipment is dedicated to the circuit. In particular the connection from the computer to the exchange is dedicated. To enable a single computer to communicate with more than one other computer at the same time, extra equipment is needed for each simultaneous call. If there are no connections all the equipment is idle but being paid for.
3. The time taken to set up the physical path can be very long in computer terms.

As high-speed connection using good-quality circuits is important for efficient computer networks, circuit switching is discounted in favour of the other methods. Circuit switching is used for some networks connecting computers-for instance, the Nordic Data Network.

Circuit switching has two advantages

1. Charges are made only for the time that a call is connected. If infrequent and short connections are all that is required, then circuit switching may be advantageous to the customer. It is expected that many slower devices, such as terminals, will be connected to national computer networks via the PSTN to gain this advantage.

2. Where a single device is used for long periods, such as a facsimile machine, circuit switching is economically advantageous. This is particularly true where digital facilities, such as X.21, are available.

The above discussion is based on the existing PSTN services offered by the PTTs. When the ISDN service is widely available, then it will be an attractive mechanism for some computer networks. Each host will be able to set up calls, use the 64K bps bandwidth, and quickly close the call, as required. The circuits will still carry packets for the end-to-end data transfer; but circuit switching will be the main link-switching mechanism. In the UK it is intended to bring all the PTT communications together into Integrated Digital Access (IDA). This will combine ISDN, X.25 networking and special digital services into a common access interface.

Message switching: To overcome problems in setting up and taking down physical circuits via exchanges, computer net-works use permanent circuits and switch the data, A partially connected network is used in which each computer has a permanent circuit to a number of its neighbours, but not to all computers on the network. An example will illustrate the basic operation of information switching where the unit of information is a message.

If the computer at A wishes to send a message to B, the message must pass through either D or C. The points on the network are called *nodes. A will* address the message to B by placing the address of B in the message header. The message and address are then sent on the circuit to D. At D the node inspects the address; if the address is 'D' the message is given to the computer; if the address is not D the message is forwarded on a circuit that the node believes will enable the message to be delivered, In this case D will forward the message to B. Thus the node at D has switched the message on to the appropriate output circuit. In this example two major characteristics of a computer network can be seen.

Addressing: The message is addressed to a remote destination and sent on the next stage of its route.

Store and forward: Each message is received into the node storage so that it can be processed as a whole unit. Usually an error check is carried out and the whole message has to be received before this can be completed. The message is then inspected for routing information so that the node can decide which output circuit to use to forward the message.

The nodes have been introduced in the network to carry out the functions of routing and store and forward, so the host computer is separated from the network operation as much as possible. The 'hosts' are the user computers which wish to use the network. Often a number of hosts will be attached to a single node.

The node computers are usually minicomputers chosen for their ability to respond in real time to the communi-cations devices. Each node receives incoming messages and stores them. When a complete message has been received the destination address is inspected so that the message can be placed on the output queue of a circuit to forward the message. If the message is for a host attached to the node, the output circuit will be the one connected to the host. If the message is for a distant host the node must forward the message to another node on the route to the distant host. While the message is in the node store, waiting to be processed or waiting for output, it is, of course, being delayed.

The link into any one node may be used to carry messages from several different computers, as may the connection between the node and host. The physical equipment involved is used more efficiently than in circuit switching as a result of this multiplexing. Message multiplexing is the most important advantage of message and packet switching computer networks.

To distinguish between message and packet switching it is necessary to understand what a message is. This has already been introduced in earlier chapters, but a more detailed discussion is given here. The easiest way of defining a message is to say that it is a unit of information which is exchanged by users of a network. This means the characteristics of a message are only dependent on the user or the application. A message could be a few bits or a file, or even a whole database. In a message-switching network the whole message is passed from one node to another as a complete entity. Compared with circuit switching, a message-switching network has the following characteristics.

1. Any computer can communicate with any other computer without having a direct physical connection.
2. Any computer can communicate with several others using the same equipment by multiplexing messages.
3. There is no delay arising from circuit set up, but messages are delayed when they pass through a node *enroute.*

The messages can be transferred between nodes, and nodes and hosts, using an *ARQ* protocol.

Characteristic 3 implies that there is no delay arising from the use of a network other than the store and forward operation of the nodes. This is true in some networks using pure datagram techniques. However, in most networks the internode protocol used within the network introduces some delays. Any network using a virtual circuit protocol, at any level, will introduce a delay when the message or packet is given to the network. In many networks the local node negotiates for resources within the network before actually forwarding a message. This is true of an X.25 network when the call is first set up, and is true of every message on the ARPA network.

A user of a message-switching network will pass the network a message, together with a destination address, and the user will receive messages as single units.

Advantages and disadvantages

The advantages of message switching, over circuit switching are: (1) The sender may dispatch the message when convenient, even if the receiver is not ready, as the network will store the message for delivery, However, if network resources run out, an undelivered message may be deleted and thus lost; this depends on the network protocols. (2) Computers can exchange information at different speeds, as the network will buffer the message. (3) Broadcasting of a message may be possible. (4) Equipment is used more efficiently. (5) Messages may be handled by priority.

Each message is treated as a single unit. However, there are also some disadvantages. (6) A very long message will hold up other, perhaps more urgent, messages as it monopolises a circuit for the duration of its transmission. (7) As a message may be very large, the node computer may not have enough memory to store it before forwarding it; in this case the message is lost. Further, this message will never be delivered as the network does not have the required resources. (8) A very large message may mono-polise the storage of a node, because it cannot be delivered, so that other messages cannot be received by this node.

Packet switching: The disadvantages of message switching relate to the possible occurrence of *large* messages, where the exact value of 'large' will depend on the network. If a network could be certain of only handling small messages, the disadvantages would disappear. The transfer of messages is a user requirement, so a network that meets user needs must be able to handle very large messages as well as small messages. The solution to these two conflicting requirements is to break the user's message into small *packets* for transfer through the network and have the packets reassembled into the message by the receiver. Note that the message header is included as the data in the first packet and that each packet has its own header. This refinement produces packet switching, which is the most widely used switching technique for computer networks.

The physical organisation of a packet-switching network is the same as for message switching. The network is a partially connected mesh of nodes. For practical reasons most wide area networks use special node computers to perform the switching, with the user computers being attached to the nodes. The term 'host' is now widely used to mean a user computer system attached to a network. The nodes are part of the network, so the hosts use a well-defined interface for accessing the node to enable data transfer across the network. By using a node separated from the host, all of the packet-switching functions, such as storage and routing, are removed from the host. However, the host still needs considerable software to handle the protocols used to access the node and to transfer data to other computers on the network.

The advantages that packet switching has over message switching are: (1) The small maximum packet size makes storage allocation and management easier in the switching nodes, sufficiently so for minicomputers to be used.(2) The multiplexing of packets enables several messages to be interleaved on one circuit, reducing the delay seen by the user. (3) The total transmission time through the network is reduced. Figure shows a message passing from A to B which would normally require 6k + d seconds to reach B, where 3k is the transmission time of the whole message on one link and d is the node delay. If the message is broken into three packets, each taking k seconds to transmit, the whole message arrives at B in 4k + d seconds. The difference increases with the number of links traversed and the size of the message.

It would appear that packet switching solves all the problems of wide area network organisation: it uses fixed highspeed lines and minicomputers for nodes; it is also more efficient and responsive than message switching. However, although packet switching is a better technique with which to implement a computer network, users still want to transfer messages. Packet switching introduces another layer of complexity and translation between the user and the physical network transporting the bits. Fortunately, the cost of processing is falling so the extra cost is outweighed by the practical advantages. A second cost, not so easily overcome, is that each packet will have its own overheads as well as those used by each message; this will reduce the efficiency of the physical circuits.

The conclusion drawn from consideration of these three switching techniques is that packet switching, especially used in a partially connected mesh of nodes with wideband circuits, is currently the best technique for wide area computer networks. Packet switching is also used in other network technologies, rather than message switching, for the same reasons.

Wide area networks have been in existence since the early 1970s. The best known example is the ARPA network in the United States. This network was established by a government research agency to link together computer centres that had contracts for government research so that research workers could share the available computing resources. The network itself also forms part of a research project to evaluate the feasibility of a large computer network, and to investigate techniques that could be used in such a network. The ARPA network has been very successful in showing that the concept of resource sharing by use of a network is feasible. One of the most noticeable advantages that the network has introduced is a mail facility. This allows each user with access to a computer on the network to exchange mail with all the other network users. The mail facility is probably one of the main sources of traffic on the ARPA network and has certainly improved the amount of communication between researchers at different sites.

The basic techniques used within the ARPA network have been influenced by the defence aspects of the research, particularly the need for a fast response and resilience to the failure of any part. The network consists of a mesh of partially connected nodes called Interface Message Processors (IMPs). Each IMP can have up to eight hosts connected to it and may be connected to up to eight other IMPs. Each IMP accepts messages from the hosts of up to 8K bits in length. The IMP breaks the message into IK bit packets which are then forwarded through the network of IMPs to the IMP attached to the destination host. This destination IMP reassembles the message before delivering it to the destination host. If a host wishes to send a message of more than 8K bits it must break the message up itself, into 8K packets, and the destination host must reassemble the message from the 8K packets. Thus the translation between messages and packets takes place at two levels. Within the network of IMPs, packets (1K) are sent individually along whichever route is best at the time, so that packets in a single message may use different routes and may arrive at the destination IMP out of sequence. The destination IMP has to reassemble the message from the packets as they arrive. However, messages passed from the host to the IMP are delivered in the same sequence to the destination host. The technology developed for the ARPANET is now used in a number of commercial wide area networks all over the world.

The British Telecom network PSS (Packet Switching Stream) is an example of a network provided by a PTT as a public service. The design requirements for such a network are different from those of the ARPA network so they have resulted in a network with different characteristics. The network topology consists of a number of *exchanges* which are also partially connected. Each exchange is connected to a number of host computers in its area. The exchanges contain the node computers, the number of node computers in each exchange depending on the number of hosts attached to the exchange. The hosts use an access protocol called X.25 to enable them to make virtual calls to other hosts. A host will give the local exchange the destination address of the host with which it wishes to communicate. The network will route the call to the destination exchange which will then complete the call to the destination host. The call is represented by information kept at all the exchanges on the route. The information is then used to forward the packets transferred on the call. Once the call has been established the hosts may exchange their own information. This is very similar to circuit switching on the PSTN although it is provided using packet-switching techniques. The PSS network techniques are different from those on the ARPA network, where each message is addressed and transferred separately. The hosts can use a single link to the PSS exchange to carry a number of virtual calls to other hosts, thus the link is used to multiplex the calls.

Radio and satellite broadcast networks: These networks differ from wide area networks in the way in which the channel is used for communication between users. Broadcast networks use a channel to which all the users are connected, so all the users receive any transmission made on the channel. At present the two types of channel in use are local radio, covering up to a few hundred kilometres, and satellite channels which are used to span very large distances.

Networks using radio and satellite channels have special problems because noise in the channel can cause errors. There is also the problem of allocating the channel for transmission. The first operational broadcast computer network was built at the University of Hawaii using local radio transmission; many of the techniques and much of the terminology derive from this first network.

Every node receives all packets transmitted on the broadcast channel. When the received packet is complete, the node checks the packet for errors and then checks the destination address. If the address of the receiver matches the packet destination address, it is accepted; otherwise it is discarded. The problems particular to a broadcast network occur in the allocation of the channel to a node for transmitting a packet. Different solutions are used for radio and satellite links. Each node is only able to communicate with each other node via the common channel, so some scheme is needed to coordinate transmission. The schemes that have been proposed and used are discussed here in increasing complexity and are compared for channel efficiency.

The simplest transmission technique is called *pure aloha;* when a node has a packet to transmit it does so immediately. Having transmitted the packet, the node waits for an acknowledgement. This is therefore a positive acknowledgement protocol. If an acknowledgement is not received within a time out period, the packet is assumed lost. Transmission collisions, which occur when two nodes transmit at the same time and thus interfere with each other's transmission, are detected by the time out mechanism. When a collision is detected, each node waits a period of time of random length before retransmitting the packet to of traffic increases, the rate of collision will increase and more retransmissions will be needed. As the older packets are retransmitted, more stations will have newer packets to transmit, causing more collisions, etc. Analysis has shown that a pure aloha scheme can only use a maximum of about 18% of the channel bandwidth. A node may transmit at any time, thus the maximum length of time the channel is wasted as a result of a collision is 2t, where t is the transmission time for one packet. The 2t period is the worst case, where one node begins transmitting just before the previous transmission is complete.

An improvement on pure aloha is *slotted aloha* in which the transmission channel time is divided into time slots of *t.* Each node is then only allowed to begin transmitting a packet at the start of a time slot. The nodes are kept in synchronisation by a time signal on the channel. Now if a collision occurs only one slot *is* wasted, so the maximum efficiency rises to about 34% of the channel capacity. When a collision is detected, a transmitter must wait for a random number of time slots before retransmitting. When the traffic is light the wait can be quite short, but as the traffic load increases the waiting period should be increased.

From the aloha schemes it can be seen that it is collisions that cause problems, so a collision avoidance mechanism should improve efficiency. In packet radio networks a scheme known as Carrier Sense Multiple Access (CSMA) is used. When a node is transmitting all other nodes can receive the transmission, so they can avoid a collision by not transmitting themselves until the channel is free. A transmission is detected by the presence of the carrier signal in the medium. When a node has a packet to transmit it looks for the carrier; if there is no carrier the packet is transmitted. If the carrier is detected the node waits for a random length delay and tries again.

Even in a radio broadcast the signal from a transmitter takes a finite amount of time to reach all the receivers in the network. When two nodes find the channel free, they may both begin transmission because neither has heard the other one. This case is most likely to happen when two stations are waiting for the channel to become free. The length of time it takes to propagate the signal to all receivers is the time band in which collisions may occur, but it is less than the total packet transmission time. As with the aloha technique, the CSMA technique can be improved by dividing the channel time into slots and only allowing the transmission of packets to begin at the start of a time slot. The slot length is set to the propagation delay, not the packet transmission time.

The CSMA technique has been further refined by modifying the action of the node when the channel is busy. When the node samples the channel again and finds it free, it transmits its packet with a probability p, or waits for a further delay of random length, with a probability (1-p). This is called persistent CSMA or p-persistent transmission. If p is high then the delay before transmission occurs is lower, but the possibility of collision increases if two stations are waiting for another station to finish. In persistent CSMA a trade off is made between channel efficiency and delay with the value of p. Channel efficiencies of about 80% may be achieved using these techniques.

Packet radio networks have a small delay between the start of a transmission and the detection of the transmission by all stations on the network. On a satellite broadcast network there is a very long delay between transmission and receiving, of the order of a quarter of a second. A satellite network operates by each transmitter sending its signal to the satellite. The satellite then broadcasts the signal to all of the Earth stations, which may be spread over a very large area. One satellite system currently used for packet switching connects nodes in England, Norway and North America using a satellite in stationary orbit over the North Atlantic. A different channel allocation technique is used on satellite broadcast networks because of the long propagation delay.

This satellite channel allocation technique involves making reservations for the future use of slots in the channel. The channel is divided into frames consisting of a number of reservation slots and a number of packet slots. Each reservation slot represents a packet slot in the second part of the frame. All ground stations are synchronised to the frame timing by the satellite transmission. During the first part of the frame the ground stations reserve slots for the packets they have ready by transmitting a marker during the reservation slot time. When the reservation slot is heard on the satellite down channel, the ground station inspects the slot to see if it contains its own marker. If so it can transmit a packet in the corresponding packet slot in the second part of the frame. This scheme uses some of the channel capacity to avoid the collisions which could reduce the network to a pure aloha scheme.

Obviously more than one ground station may attempt to reserve a particular packet slot by transmitting during the reservation slot time. There are a number of algorithms to overcome this, including allocating some slots to busy stations. Thus if a station successfully obtained a packet slot in the last frame, the same slot is allocated to that station in the next frame without competition. If an allocated slot is not used then the slot is open for competition in the following frame. Usually there are some slots that all stations can compete for in every frame. Another mechanism involves using a central allocation station to which each station sends its requirements and the central station allocates the slots. This has two disadvantages: firstly, the central station becomes a weakness in the network reliability, and secondly, the delay between requesting an allocation and receiving the allocation may be of the order of 1 or 2 seconds before the packet can be transmitted. A chapter in the book by Kuo is dedicated to broadcast satellite protocols.

Local area networks: A local, or private, network is a communication system connecting computers in a small geographical area, say less than a few kilometres between the furthest points. The network is wholly owned and run by one administration. There are currently two basic types of technology used on such a network: these are cable, or bus, technology and ring technology.

Whereas wide area networks and satellite networks use nodes to separate the internal network switching from the user hosts, local networks are meant to be as cheap as possible and so the separate node computer is omitted. In both local network technologies all the computers are directly attached to the transmission medium by a special interface, and all the interfaces receive all the packets. The difference between a ring and a bus system is the way in which the channel is allocated. Local networks are designed for use in local computing by allowing the interconnection of very small computers, such as microprocessors, personal workstations and peripheral devices. If the local network is to be useful, the cost of the computer interfaces into the network channel has to be low compared with the cost of the computer or peripheral, and microprocessors are very cheap in computer terms. A widely forecast use of local networks is connecting word processors within a set of offices for the exchange of information and electronic mail. The cost constraints, the limited processing power of the small computers and the protocols used on a local network are different from those used in wide area networks. A local network usually has a very high bandwidth channel of between I and 10 MHz and a very low error rate say one bit in several million might be corrupted. These characteristics permit the use of simple protocols. The lowest level protocol for using the transmission medium is built into the computer interface.

Cable or bus networks: These networks usually use a length of coaxial cable, or an existing cable such as that used for closed circuit television (CCTV). The medium is used in a broadcast fashion, exactly as described in the previous section on broadcast networks. The channel allocation techniques vary slightly on the theme of the CSMA techniques, or on a centralised slot allocation. The most popular broadcast local network is the Ethernet system developed by Xerox. The Ethernet principles can be used on any broadcast medium: radio, telephone lines, coaxial cable and optical fibres have all been used successfully. The Ethernet uses a base band signal, rather than a modulated signal, to simplify the broadcast transmitter and receiver, with a modified CSMA channel access technique. To obtain the maximum efficiency from the broadcast medium an Ethernet transmitter can listen to its own broadcast to detect a collision and abort the transmission. This extra complexity is known as CSMACD or listen-while-talk. As with the other CSMA techniques a station does not begin transmitting until the broadcast medium is free. Two stations waiting for another station to finish a transmission will begin transmitting together, and thus interfere with each other. The collision is detected by the stations and they both abort the transmission immediately. To enforce the protocol a station that aborts a transfer then jams the ether. After a collision each station waits for a random time before trying again.

The CSMA-CD technique enables the Ethernet system to obtain up to 95% of the broadcast channel bandwidth. The improvement in performance over ordinary CSMA is due to the stopping of transmission as soon as a collision is detected. Note that no slots are used so a network-wide timing signal is not required. The transceiver handles all of the CSMACD access, including the retries and delay calculation which is varied with the traffic load. Thus only complete, and checked, packets are passed up to the station interface and only one request is made for a packet to be sent. The checksum generation and checking are carried out within the hardware: bad packets are discarded. A time out mechanism is used to retransmit packets that may have been lost as a result of errors.

Ring networks: The ring technique originated in the USA. The idea was then developed in parallel at Cambridge University in the UK and at two research centres in the USA. The version developed at Cambridge is known as the Cambridge ring in the UK. The computer interface is divided into two parts: the repeater and the interface proper. A ring uses a twisted pair of wires as the transmission medium. However, to improve reliability, the repeater is powered from the ring and electrically isolated from the computer interface, so four wires are used to connect the repeaters. The four wires are used as two pairs for signalling and carry sufficient power for the repeaters. In this way the computer can be switched off and removed from the ring without switching off the repeater. With the ring the medium is terminated at each station, whereas in the cable network it is not. Each station is represented by a repeater, several of which are then connected together into a ring. The repeater is a simple device containing a shift register and some logic to detect certain conditions in the information being passed around the ring. The repeater normally passes any information received on to the next repeater, so transmission only occurs in one direction. When a station transmits data, the repeater transmits the information from the station instead of the information received from the previous repeater.

Slotted ring: There are slight differences in the channel allocation mechanism used in the Cambridge ring and in those rings developed in the USA. In the Cambridge ring a fixed-size mini-packet is used which constantly circulates in the ring, and a special station called a monitor is used to generate and maintain the mini-packet and provide the power for the repeaters. In the American versions a variable-size packet is used which may be lost and regenerated as required by each repeater. The current format of the Cambridge mini-packet. Note that only 16 bits of information are carried in a ring mini-packet whereas the broadcast network packet may contain several hundred bytes. The assembly of information into a block has to be done by the computer. The monitor station also provides a buffer if the ring is not physically long enough to hold a complete mini-packet. The monitor performs a check on the mini-packet each time it passes to ensure that it is intact, and to replace it if not. The monitor is an obvious weakness in the Cambridge ring design so far as reliability is concerned; however, experience so far has shown that monitor failures are rare. The advantage of the monitor is that the repeaters can be very simple as well as cheap, which is the purpose of a local network.

To use the ring to send a packet of information, the station will wait until an empty mini-packet is detected by the repeater. When the full/empty bit in the mini-packet passes the repeater it is set to one. If the packet was already full no change has been made to the bit; if the packet was empty (full/empty bit = 0) the mini-packet is now reserved by this station, The repeater will use this mini-packet if the full/empty bit was received as 0. The addresses of the source and destination stations are placed in the address fields followed by the next 16 bits of the information that the station wishes to send; these are placed in the data field from the station buffer. The reserved mini-packet then travels round to all the other stations on the ring. Each station has a source select register in which an address is placed. If the source address in a mini-packet matches the contents of the source select register, and the destination address matches the station address, the data field is copied into the station receive buffer and the accept status is set at the end of the packet. If the packet is refused, or the destination station is busy, the destination repeater will set the appropriate value in the status bits at the end of the mini-packet. No other change is made by the receiving repeater, and all other repeaters will pass on the mini-packet unchanged. Special values which can be used in the source select register are: All ones, which means accept any source station address, and all zeros, which means do not accept the data from any mini-packets.

When the mini-packet returns to the sending station the full/empty bit is reset to 0 and the status bits are checked to see if the information was accepted. As an error check, the station also reads back the 16 data bits and checks them against the data in its buffer. Having reset the full/empty bit, the station must now wait for another empty mini-packet before it can send the next 16 bits of information. In this way the now empty packet becomes available to successive stations around the ring and the packet slot is allocated in a round robin fashion.

The variable nature of packet traffic in a local network makes it difficult to design a system that will provide a very fast response, especially when there is little traffic, and yet not become overloaded or unfair when the traffic becomes heavy. The broadcast techniques provide a low delay, especially in low-volume traffic, as the transmitter can usually send a packet as soon as one is available. However, as the volume of traffic increases, the broadcast system suffers from collisions and longer delays which can eventually lead to an unstable situation. In the slotted ring the channel is allocated by means of a round robin mechanism so collisions never occur, and during a burst of traffic each station is able to continue transmitting with only a larger delay. During periods of low traffic volume the ring does introduce a delay while a station waits for the empty packet to come round.

Proponents of both systems argue that because of the very high bandwidth available on the channel, and the low processing power of the computers attached to the local network, the volume of traffic is nearly always low in a broadcast network and the delay is negligible in a ring.

Token Ring: The token ring attempts to provide the advantages of broadcast access in low-volume traffic periods, with the inherent sharing of the slotted ring during high-volume traffic periods. The physical topology of the ring is the same, but instead of a circulating mini-packet there is a circulating token. Any host requiring access to the ring waits for the token to arrive; it then changes the token to indicate that a packet is following. The modified token is then followed immediately by the data packet, which can be of any size up to some system maximum. All hosts detect the modified token and examine the packet to see if it is addressed to them; if it is the packet is copied off the ring. The receiving host still sends the packet on though, so the data packet goes all the way round the ring to the sender. The sender takes the packet off the ring. Normally the sender receives the front of the data packet before it has finished transmitting the rest of the packet, owing to the short length of the ring. When the receiver detects the end of the data packet it marks its status by changing the last few bits, as in the Cambridge ring mini-packet; thus the sender knows if the packet was accepted or not. Immediately the sender has finished the packet it puts a token on the ring so another host may have a go.

The token ring is a simple idea, but it is more complex than the Cambridge ring and the interfaces are more expensive. The initialise sequence which is required to start the ring is quite complex as the token has to be put on the ring to start data transfer; of course there can only be one token. The mechanisms for detecting duplicate tokens and lost tokens, without the use of a monitor station, add to the cost of the computer interfaces. IBM carried out extensive tests and simulations of all the local area network technologies, and decided that the token ring was the best available. The company now intends to use the token ring as the basis of its local area network products.

Computer Professionals for Social Responsibility (CPSR): An organization of computer professionals concerned with the computers might have on society.

Computer Programmer: A computer professional who designs and/or writes computer programs.

Computer Science: The study of computer technology, programming, algorithms etc. Computer Science degrees are offered by many universities and institutes of technology.

Computer + Science Network (CSNET): A computer-science research network that merged with BITNET to create the Corporation for Research and Educational Networking (CREN).

Computerese: The language spoken by computer professionals.

Concatenation: The linking of two or more strings of characters into one string.

Concurrent Processing: The processing of more than one task at any one time by using time division techniques.

Condensed Print: A printed character that is smaller (in the horizontal and/or vertical) than a normal character.

Conditioning: Used in reference to transmission lines and power supply. Each may be "conditioned" so as to improve performance, reliability or regulation.

Conductor: A particular type of wire, such as copper.

Conferencing: (adj) Said of software that enables many users to engage in a more or less public, written conversation, either in real time.

Configuration: The way in which the internal resources (particularly memory) of a computer are organised and allocated. The "configuration" of a computer may also refer to hardware.

Configuration File: A special file, usually only read during the boot process, that defines the organisation and allocation of the computer's resources, particularly memory.

Config.Sys: Under MS-DOS this is a configuration file, used to define certain parameters of the operating system environment. The Config.Sys file is only read during booting. An example of a typical Config.Sys file is shown below,

BUFFERS=30

FILES=30

DEVICE=DMDRVR.BIN

DEVICE=C:\DOS\ANSI.SYS

DEVICE=C:\DOS\SMAIRTDRV.S 1024

DEVICE=C\DOS\RAMDRIVE.SYS 1024 128

This config.sys file allocates 30 areas of memory to, be used as buffers; allows the operating system to interact with up to 30 files at any one time; loads DMDRVR.BIN, a disk manager; loads DOS\ANSI.SYS, a software utility for the computer keyboard; loads DOS\SMARTDRV.SYS, a mem-ory management application; loads DOS\RAMDRIVE.SYS 1024 128, creating a RAM Drive of 1MB with 128B sectors.

Connection: There are different types, or levels, of connection to the Internet, ranging from a direct network connection, through SLIP or PPP dial-up access, to character-based shell-account dial-up access, and simple e-mail gateways to the Net.

Connection dosed by foreign host: A message during a telnet or other remote login session that tells you that the host you've logged in to has closed the connection.

Connection Control Language (CCL): An Apple Talk scripting language for controlling modem functions.

Connectionless communication: A form of communication between applications in which data can be requested and supplied during intermittent connections.

Connection-oriented communication: A form of communication between applications in which all data is exchanged during a single connection.

Connect time: The amount of time you spend connected to your service provider. Many providers charge a fee based on your connect time, others are flatrate providers.

Consortium for School Networking (CoSN): A non-profit organization that studies the uses of networking in K-12 schooling.

Conspiracy: The Internet is home to many conspiracy theorists and provides an excellent means for the sharing of theories, rumors, and evidence. Don't try to keep all the conspiracies straight or you'll lose your mind. Some of them deal with the creation and "control" of the Internet itself.

Constant: A designated item in a computer program that does not change during program execution. For example a programmer may make the following statement in the program header, P = 3.14159. This enables the programmer to refer to the value "P" throughout the program rather than 3.14159. This is a good programming tactic as it ensures that the same value is always referred to. As well, if it is decided to change the value of "P" only one line of code need be altered.

Consumable: Any hardware accessory, for example, printer ribbons, toner, paper etc, that has to be purchased on a regular basis.

Contention: This is a word used in data communications and computer networks, to describe when two devices attempt to use the same transmission path at the same time.

Contiguous: Another word for adjoining. The word cotiguous is often used to describe the layout of sectors on a hard disk.

Continuons Form Paper: Computer paper that has been pre-perforated and can be separated into individual sheets after printing. A popular print medium since, once threaded, the entire stack of paper will feed through the computer printer. Continuous Form Paper is transported through the printer by the use of sprocket holes on a detachable margin.

Control bus: The channel within a computer along which control signals (signals that control a device or routine) are carried.

Control character: A special character, usually nonprinting, that starts or stops a computer function.

Control Key: On most key-boards, a key that is used in combination with other keys to invoke a particular task.

Conversational Monitor System (CMS): The command-line interface of IBM's VM operating system.

Cookie: A fortune cookie program that spits out a different fortune every time you run it. Some systems run cookie as part of their startup or login procedure.

Coordinating Committee for Intercontinental Research Networks (CCIRN): A committee that coordinates research networks in North America and Europe.

Co-Processor: A special purpose microprocessor that is used in conjunction with the main microprocessor. Co-processors are typically used for mathematical operations. Also known as a Math Co-Processor.

Copy: An operating system or software application command that produces a copy of a data file.

Copyleft: The General Public License carried by Free Software Foundation software (such as GNU). It grants reuse ,and reproduction rights to anyone and everyone.

Copy Protection: A feature of some software packages that prevents the user front making copies of the software. This is to prevent software piracy, although it is an annoying feature for many legitimate users of the software.

Copyright: Designates owner-ship of a proprietary work, such as a computer program, a painting, a journal article, a photograph or a book. Copyright rests with the owner of the original material. In the case of a tangible asset such as a photograph this may be a photonegative, with an intangible asset the "original material" may be difficult to define. Such instances are now covered by legal protection of "Intellectual Property".

Core: (n) 1. RAM, on UNIX and some IBM machines; 2. The name of a file that appears in your UNIX directory after a core dump. This file contains everything that was in memory at the time of the dump.

Core dump: (In) 1. A copy of the contents of memory, dumped into a file when an unre-coverable error occurs; 2. A brain dump.

Corporation for Research and Educational Networking (CREN): An organization formed by the merger of BITNET and CSNET. CREN can be reached via gopher at info.educom.edu.

Corrupted: (adj) Said of a file, block of data, or other communication, damaged transmission.

cp: The UNIX *copy file* command.

cpio: A UNIX command that makes whole directories into a single file, for easy transportation.

CP/M: This was one of the first disk operating systems, it was written in 1975 by Gary Kidall, the founder of Digital Research Corporation. CP/M (Control Program for Micro computers) has been widely used in PCs based on the Intel 8080 and Zilog Z80 microprocessors. The advent of CP/M and other disk operating systems enabled designers to get around the limitation imposed by small amounts of RAM and ROM. Operating System functions that were infrequently required could be retrieved from disk when necessary and did not require a permanent allocation of RAM or ROM.

.cpt: The extension of a file compressed with Compact Pro, a Macintosh program.

CPU: Abbreviation for Central Processing Unit, the main brain of any computer. The CPU provides the fundamental command and instruction environment for the computer and contains a processor, registers, a Control Unit (abbreviation CU) which controls the execution of a program, a clock and an Arithmetic Logic Unit (abbreviation ALU) which performs mathematical operations and comparisons. A CPU that is contained on a single chip is called a microprocessor. The basic outline of CPU operation may be listed as follows,

Instructions and data for a program are loaded into memory (RAM) and/or registers. The Control Unit is instructed to start executing the program starting at a particular address (sec Program Counter). Instructions are obeyed from consecutive commands unless an instruction is encountered which changes the sequence of operations. The CPU continues with this process until a stop or interrupt instruction is encountered.

CR: Abbreviation for carriage return. This term is typewriter jargon and is used with reference to printers and word processing page formats.

Cracker: One who breaks into computer systems. What many people in the real world call a hacker.

Cracking: The act of breaking into a computer system.

Crack root: (v) To break into the root account of a UNIX machine and, most likely, use the root privileges to break into other accounts.

Crippleware: Shareware that lacks a useful or even crucial functionality, in order to entice you Into registering as an owner to obtain the uncrippled version of the program.

Crlf: A combination of two characters that on some computer systems constitutes a newline.

Crosspost: (n) A Usenet article posted simultaneously to more than one newsgroup.

Cross-post: (v) To post a Usenet article to several newsgroups at once. This takes up less disk space than posting it separately and repeatedly.

Crosstalk: Interference between two wires in a cable.

CrossTalk: A communications and terminal emulation program for DOS and Windows.

Cryptography: The study of codes and ciphers and other security issues.

C shell: A common flavor of UNIX shells.

.cshrc: A startup file for the UNIX C shell.

CSLIP: *Compressed Serial Line Internet* Protocol, a faster version of SLIP in which Internet address information is compressed.

CSO: *Computing Services Office,* a system for searching campus telephone and address listings, reachable by gopher.

CSO name server: A searchable white pages listing of real names and associated e-mail addresses, usually reached via gopher.

The Cuckoo's Egg: A book by Clifford Stoll describing how he tracked East German crackers breaking into a system at Lawrence Berkeley Labs at the University of California at Berkeley.

CU: Abbreviation for Control Unit. A part of the Central Processing Unit (CPU) that provides sequential control over the execution of a program.

Cursor: The character used on a computer monitor to indicate where the next piece of data entry will occur.

Cut and Paste: The process of taking part of a file and inserting it into another place in the same file or into another file.

CUSeeMe: *(see-you-see-me)* A new Internet protocol for synchronous video and sound communication.

Cyber: A prefix overused to indicate a connection to computers, networks, technology, or futurism.

Cyberdelics: 1. Mindaltering effects brought about by computer technology (as opposed to hallucinogenic drugs); 2. Eye-bending screen savers.

Cybernaut: A traveler in cyberspace, someone who uses their Internet connection to explore the furthest realms of cyberspace.

Cyberpunk: A largely hype-driven category of popular culture at the crossroads of computer technology, science fiction, and youth culture.

Cyberspace: A term, popularized by author William Gibson, for the shared imaginary reality of computer networks, Some people use cyberspace as a synonym for the Internet.

Cycle power: (v) To turn a computer off and then on again.

Cyclic Redundancy Check: An error detection scheme used in data communications that uses a polynomial function to generate parity checking characters.

Cyclic redundancy check (CRC): An error-detection technique used during file transfers and other forms of data transmission.

D

Daemon: *(day-min)* In UNIX and other operating systems, a program that runs all, the time, in the background, waiting for things to do (possibly from Maxwell's Demon).

Daisy chain: A network architecture, also called *bus topology* in which all nodes are connected to a single cable.

Daisy wheel printer: A type of impact printer that uses a print wheel with characters embedded on a series of spokes or stems radiating out froth the central core.. The term "daisy wheel" is used since the wheel resembles the flowering head of a daisy, where the characters are embedded on the ends of the petals. During printer operation the daisy wheel is rotated until the appropriate character appears under the strike hammer and the relevant character is imprinted, via a ribbon, on to the paper.

Although daisy wheel printers produce very well defined characters they are often inconvenient to use since each daisy wheel has only one font. If more than one font is required for a document then it is a tiresome task to have to stop the printer, change wheels, and continue with the print job. The characters embedded on the wheel are not necessarily arranged in alphabetical order.

Dark fiber: Unused cable in the fiberoptic network.

DARPA: *Defense Advanced Research Projects* the official name of ARPA during the 1980s and early 1990s.

Data: Any computer usable information. This may be numerical, for example the depth of snow at a skiresort over the past fifty years is numerical data; it may be textual, for example a list of customers; or it may be graphical, for example the input from a graphic scanner. Data may be entered into the computer via the keyboard, secondary storage, for example, a disk or tape, via another computer or via a peripheral device such as a scanner, or a remote sensing device, for example, a weather station.

Database: A collection of data, usually related in some manner. For example a list of customer names, addresses and telephone numbers constitutes a database. Another example is a payroll listing of employee names, employee numbers, bank details, tax file numbers, pay rates etc. The telephone directory is a classic example of a database, however the name "database" is generally not used until the data has been entered into and stored by the computer. Database software applications are commonly found on mainframe computers and are popular, useful,' items for personal computer users.

Database Management System: A collection of software applications that allow the computer user to setup, maintain and manipulate a database. Management tasks may include controlling access to the database, or sections of it, extracting data selectively from different parts of the database, financial and statistical analysis. Usually abbreviated to DBMS.

Database Query Language: A command and/or programming language, forming an integral part of a database package. A query language allows the user to extract and manipulate data from the database based on user defined criteria, Data, Bus. A set of wires or printed circuit tracks that is used for transferring data within the computer and its peripherals.

Data bits: In asynchronous data transmission, the bits between a start bit (and sometimes a parity bit) and a stop bit, the only bits actually carrying data. There are usually seven or eight data bits, depending on the size of a character, or byte.

Data bits is therefore one of the settings you have to specify on your modem to make a connection. Usually 7 or 8, it depends on the, modem you're calling.

Data block: A unit of data sent from one device to another.

Data bus: The channel within a computer along which communication signals are carried.

Data channel: Any channel over which data is sent in the form of a signal.

Data Communications: A communications system used primarily, but not necessarily exclusively, for the transmission of data. Data communications has become an increasingly important revenue source to common carriers over the past 20 years. Since the mid-1970s most common carriers in the USA have made more money out of data communication than voice communication. Increasingly, air-waves and cables are congested by machines talking to other machines. The process of transmitting data from one computer to another, or from any device to another device.

Data Communications Equipment: Any equipment involved in a communications link.

Data Compression: This refers to the compressing of data prior to transmission in order to save transmission time, and therefore money. There are several methods of compression, one is to eliminate any unnecessary spaces and to condense repeated characters to a code.

Data Dictionary: These are used in Systems Analysis, program and database design. A data dictionary, also called MetaData lists all the attributes of the data that is to constitute the data fields of a database.

A data dictionary provides c and relates organisational activities to program design. Some countries have formal standards for data dictionaries.

Data Element: A single entity within a dataset or database. For example, a person's tax file number would be a data element of a payroll database.

Data encryption key (DEK): An element of key encryption that is used to encrypt and decrypt data.

Data encryption standard (DES): A security protocol defined by the U.S. government.

Data Entry: The process of entering data into a computer. Traditionally this has been a manual process, performed by computer operators but much of this work is now automated. For example, stock control in many large shops is now achieved by direct data entry from cash register transactions. Similarly, bank account records are updated by transactions conducted by members of the public through automatic teller machines (ATMs).

Data/fax modem: A modem that can transmit raw data or a fax image.

Datagram: The basic unit of data transmission across a network, containing a header and the data itself. The header describes the data, its destination, and its relationship to other datagrams.

Datagram: Delivery Protocol (DDP) An AppleTalk protocol that handles the routing of datagrams over an AppleTalk network.

Data Integrity: This refers to the reliability of any particular data. For example, data on the world's climate from 500 years ago would be very sketchy, and unsuitable for indepth analysis. In another example, the data collected during a vehicle count on Sydney Harbour Bridge may be of doubtful integrity if it is known that one of the recorders had an intermittent fault.

Data link: The device that enables data transmission; 2. An active connection for data transmission.

Data link layer: The second layer of the OSI Model that deals with transmission of data frames from node to node.

Data Processing: The manipulation of data to produce usable information for example, the processing of time sheet information to Produce a list of payroll bank transfers.

Data Service: A communications network operated by common carriers, which otters high speed transmission of digital data, mostly to and from computers and peripherals such as remote sensors, telemetry devices etc.

Data Source: Any organisation, person, place or device that generates a dataset or database. For example, the data source for information (data) on world food prices may he the United Nations, the data source on Australian household incomes may be a professional pollster or the Australian Bureau of Statistics.

Data stream: A series of data blocks sent from one device to another.

Data Terminal Equipment: The terminating hardware involved in the transmission process. Usually located in an organisation's premises.

Data Transfer Rate: The rate, in kilobytes or megabytes per second, at which data can be read/written from/to CDROM, disk, tape etc.

Data Verification: In many applications, particularly databases, it is essential to verify that the data being entered in to the database is of the right type, length etc. For example, a payroll database would record, amongst other things, an employee's address and postcode. A professionally designed database would cheek that the entry for postcode is totally numeric and exactly four digits long. An entry for postcode of "abcd" would be rejected, as would "31889". Checks such as this are known as data verification. A more thorough verification would also ensure that the postcode is within the accepted range of numbers.

Another aspect of data verification is to check for duplication of entries. Using a payroll database as an example, this database would record an employee number and tax file number for each employee. Obviously there could never be more than one person with the same employee number, or the same tax file number, Each new entry to the database would need to be checked in this manner against existing database entries. However, most data items in a database would riot need to be checked for duplication. For example, surname, first names, address, postcode etc can all be quite legitimately duplicated.

DCE: Data communications equipment or Distributed Computing Environment.

DDCMP: Digital Data Communications Message Protocol.

DDN: Defense Data Network.

DDN NIC: Defense Data Network Network Information Center.

DDP: Datagrarn Delivery Protocol.

DEC: *(deck) Digital Equipment Corporation,* manufacturer of VAX (and before that PDP-11) boxes and the VMS operating system.

Deadly Embrace: A clash of hardware/software that results in a system lockup. Often the only solution to this situation lies in the Power On/Off switch or rebooting.

Debugging: Jargon for fault finding, usually in software but also in hardware. A phrase first used by computer developers in the US Navy in 1945. At this time a US Navy prototype computer ground to a halt and after a long period of investigation the fault was found to be a moth that had died amongst the wiring panels of the computer. Getting the computer up-and-running again was a merely a matter of debugging.

DEchead: *(deck-head)* 1. An employee of Digital Equipment Corporation; 2. A Deadhead (Grateful Dead fan) employee of DEC.

Decimal Numbering: A numbering system which uses a cycle of ten digits as the basis for the counting procedure.

Decision Support System: A database system whose purpose is largely geared towards decision making. A Decision Support System is not necessarily an online, working database. It may draw data from the day-to-day activities of the organisation, but it is generally not involved in actual transaction processing.

Declaration: A technique used in some programming languages where the programmer must "declare", that is notify, the software/compiler/translator of the variables that will be used in the program and their type.

DECnet: *(deck-net)* Network protocols designed for VAX and PDP-11 computers, used by Digital Equipment Corporation operating systems instead of TCP/IP.

DECnet/DNA: DEC's implementation of DNA (Digital Network Architecture).

DECnet tunnel: A protocol for packaging AppleTalk datagrams within DECnet packets.

Decrypt: To remove the encryption from a file or e-mail message and make it readable.

Decryption key: In key encryption, a key used to decipher an encrypted message and make it readable.

Dedicated: (adj) Assigned to a single task or able to perform only a single task.

Dedicated line: A telephone line dedicated to telecommunications.

Deep hack: The extreme state of concentration, bordering on a trance, that hackers enter after long hours of hacking.

Default: A group of settings applied to a computer in the absence of specific instructions from the user or software application. For example, the default setting for reading and writing data in a spreadsheet package may he a specific hard disk directory, the default setting for text blocks in a word processing package may be 90mm, the default data transmission settings for communications between two computers may be 9600 baud.

Default route: An entry in a routing table indicating where to route packets intended for destinations not otherwise listed in the table.

Defense Data Network (DDN): The network of networks used by the U.S. military, connecting with the, Internet in some places and not in others.

Defense Data Network Network Information Center (DDN NIC): The

Network Information Center for the DDN, a source of information as well as an administrative authority over the DDN.

Defense Information Systems Agency (DISA): The U.S. government agency that, oversees the Defense Data Network.

Delete key: A key used in most environments to erase the character that the cursor or insertion point is on or just before. On some systems, Delete erases the character just typed or to the left of the cursor.

Delimiter: A character or symbol that indicates a break between two pieces of information, items in a table, or fields in a database.

Delurk: *(dee-lurk,* v) To post to a list or newsgroup for the first time.

Demon: A routine in a program that waits until it is needed (possibly from Maxwell's Demon):

Depew, Dick: The inventor of ARMM, a roboposting utility designed to retroactively cancel off-topic Usenet posts. Depew's 'bot had a serious flaw and followed up its own posts, eventually bringing down part of the internet in sorcerers apprentice mode.

Deprecated: (adj) Being phased out in favour of a new standard,

DES: Data encryption standard.

Despew: (v) From [Dick] Depew, to robopost reams of junk to the Net.

Developer: A software publisher.

Device: A software, utility program used to enhance or change the default settings of a computer, particularly with reference to how memory is managed.

Device Driver: A software utility program used to enhance or change the default settings of a computer, particularly with reference to how memory is managed. Also a utility program that describes the protocol for accessing a particular part of computer hardware.

/dev/null: On UNIX boxes, the null device. Data piped to /dev/null disappears. People posting controversial articles to Usenet sometimes add the notice "flames to /dev/null."

Dhrystone: This is an industry standard that measures the number of times a particular task, or group of tasks, can be executed per second. Dhrystones are used as a standardised measure of processing speed, for example, the Intel 80386 microprocessor running at 16MHz has been rated at 6000-7000 Dhrystones.

Dialog Box: A menu that poses a number of questions or alternatives to the user, the user responds to all or some of the questions and then returns to the main menu or the previous/next task.

Dial up: (v) To use a modem to call up another computer or network and log in to it.

Dial-up: (adj) Said of an Internet access that requires the user to connect via a modem.

Dial-up account: An Internet account on a host machine that you must dial up with your modem to use.

DIALOG Information Retrieval Database: A commercial online database service with hundreds of databases and millions of records. To connect to DIALOG, telnet to dialog.com.

Dictionary flame: A flame that focuses on someone's use of a particular word or their vocabulary, a weak sort of flame that indicates that the flamer has nothing substantial to say against the flamee.

Digest: (n) A collection of mailing list posts, sent out as one message.

Digestified: (adj) Turned into a digest. Not all mailing lists are available in a digestified form.

Digital: (adj) Representing values as discrete bits. CD is a digital medium because the second or other information is digitized, converted into bits) and then stored. A CD player converts the digital information encoded on the CD into an analog signal sent to the amplifier.

Digital Computer: A computer that uses digital techniques, most computers use this approach.

Digital Data Communications Message Protocol (DDCMP): A DECnet data link protocol that can handle a both synchronous and asynchronous links.

Digital Equipment Corporation (DEC): Manufacturer of VAX (and before that PDP-11) boxes and the VMS operating system.

Digital Metropolitan Service: A digital data communications network operated by Telecom Australia in major cities. It provides a direct digital connection between data sources.

Digital Network Architecture (DNA): A set of protocols for network architecture.

Digital Transmission: A transmission method in which data is transmitted in binary form (0 and 1) rather than in analog form. Digital Transmission is only practicable over short distances (for example, within a Local Area Network). See also Analog Transmission, Binary Numbering, Local Area Network.

Digitizer: A hardware/software combination that will scan a piece of artwork in very fine detail. Digitizers are often used in cartography to produce computer based images of geographic/demographic information.

DIP: Abbreviation for Dual In-Line Package. This is a "conventional" chip (integrated circuit), having pins (connectors) on both sides.

DIP Switch: A small toggle switch, used on many hardware devices, including computers, to set different options. For example, on a printer, the maximum paper width, on a computer, the amount of RAM available. DIP switches are not changed very often and for this reason are usually located within the hardware case, or out of the way where they won't he accidentally knocked.

Directed information: Information intended for a particular recipient, such as private email.

Directory: An organizing structure for files. In most operating systems, directories can themselves be organized hierarchically into a "tree" of parent and children directories.

Direct Access: Data storage where each and every data field can be accessed directly without first traversing the memory areas occupied by other data. A hard disk, a floppy disk, an LP record and a compact disk offer direct access, whereas a computer tape, a video or audio cassette do not. When access is required to a particular item on the cassette it is necessary to wind through the intervening items (programs or songs). Direct access is also called random access, since any item can be accessed at random.

Directory Access Protocol (DAP): An X.500 protocol governing communication between a Directory User Agent and a Directory System Agent.

Direct Access Storage Device: Any storage device that uses direct (random) access methods, for example, hard disk, floppy disk, CD-ROM etc. Abbreviation DASD).

Direct Memory Access: A memory management technique where data can be loaded into RAM without the direct involvement of the CPU. Abbreviation DMA.

Directory: A part of secondary storage that is allocated for storage of related files. A directory can be compared to a manual filing system and considered as a filing cabinet in a room full of similar filing cabinets. Each filing cabinet has a specific purpose and is labelled and used accordingly. The drawers of each filing cabinet can, of course, also be considered as directories, as can individual hangers within each drawer, and the folders within each hanger. For example, a company may store all information relating to its payroll database under "Payroll"; customers in the state of Western Australia under "WA; administration under "Admin". In this way files that are related to each other, or which have a common theme, are kept together in a distinct, and conveniently addressable, storage location.

Directories are created by the operating system via direct commands from the user or via software applications, for example MS-DOS uses the command MKDIR to create a directory.

Directory listing: A summary list of available files, possibly including file sizes, attributes, date and time of creation or last changes, and the owner, where appropriate.

Directory service: A database of sites and usernames that enables users to locate other users, hosts, and services.

Directory Structure: The hierarchical arrangement of different directories on secondary storage media. The directory structure indicates the relationship, if any, of the directories to one another. Several software utilities will display the directory structure on screen or provide a hard copy of it.

Directory System Agent (DSA): X.500 software that serves directory information to Directory User Agents.

Directory User Agent (DUA): X.500 software that queries a Directory System Agent for directory information.

DISA: Defense Information Systems Agency.

Disable: To temporarily disconnect or make non-functional (without necessarily shutting off).

Disaster Recovery: A management strategy for recovering full operation after a disaster (for example, fire or flood damage). This usually involves making regular backup copies of everything and storing them offsite.

Disclaimer: The line in some sig blocks asserting that the opinions of the writer are not necessarily those of the organization providing her internet access.

Discordianism: The principles of the Discordian Society, as set clown in the *Principia* Discordia and other sacred (or profane) texts.

Discordian Society: Followers of the goddess Eris (or Discordia), a mostly farcical organization spawned from Robert Anton Wilson's *Illuminati*! trilogy.

Discrete Components: Much of the electronic circuitry of a computer is contained within integrated circuits, however for many tasks individual, physically separate, electronic components are used. For example, part of the power control circuitry may consist of transistors and associated components, all of which can be visually identified on the circuit board. These are said to be discrete components. See also Integrated Circuit.

Discussion group: Any online group of likeminded people who may communicate via a mailing list, in a newsgroup, on an IRC channel, etc.

Disk: A generic name for magnetic storage media, using flat, circular platters.

Disk Controller: The electronic circuitry that is the interface between a disk drive and the CPU. This is often an integral part of the motherboard but may also be a separate circuit board.

Disk Drive: An electromechanical device that reads and writes data to a floppy or hard disk. In mainframe computers disk drives are located externally from the central processor cabinet, in personal computers they may share the same "can". The disk itself may form an integral part of the disk drive, these are often called "fixed disks" or "nonremovable disks".

Diskette: A generic name for magnetic storage media, using flat, circular platters, generally only used when referring to floppy disks. The word "diskette" was initiated by IBM with the introduction of its 3740 Terminal, which incorporated a "diskette drive", in 1972.

Disk Failure: A failure of a hard or floppy disk drive and/ or the disk itself. As these are electromechanical devices, it is to be expected that all disks and disk drives will ultimately fail. The mean time between failure (MTBF) of a hard disk is estimated at 20000 hours.

Disk Operating System: A method of computer operation where the computer does not have a permanent record of operating system instructions. The operating system is loaded every time the power is turned on (from secondary storage, floppy disk or hard disk). Such computers are said to have a "disk operating system" (abbreviation DOS). Although "disk operating system" is a generic term for any computer using the methods described, the phrase "disk operating system" has become synonymous with IBM personal computers running under PC-DOS and IBM compatible personal computers running under Microsoft DOS (also known as MS-DOS).

Disk Optimiser: A utility program that keeps a check on fragmentation of data files. The disk optimiser copies files and reallocates disk space as required so as to reduce fragmentation.

Disk Pack: A secondary storage device in a mainframe or minicomputer. A disk pack is a collection of hard disks (each one called a platter) used as a single, addressable memory location. Typically there will be 812 platters in one disk pack. The upper and lower surface of a disk pack are generally not used since the likelihood of mechanical damage (due to handling) is high. This means that if there are 11 platters in a disk pack then there are only 20 "usable surfaces". Some disk packs are a fixed part of the associated disk drive, others are removable, so that a disk pack can be removed from the drive and another one inserted. These are known as Removable Disk Packs, basically a hard disk with the added convenience of take-away data. Disk Pack sizes are in the range 20MB- 80MB. See also Winchester Disk.

Disk server: A network program that enables a computer to use a disk drive on another computer (or a partition of such a disk drive) as if it were a local disk drive.

Distinct TCP/IP Tools: A set of Internet tools for Windows sold by Distinct Corporation.

Distributed computing: An approach to computing that allows applications to run the same way across different types of networks,

Distributed Computing Environment (DCE): A set of standards for servers, interfaces, and protocols promoted by the Open Software Foundation to enable distributed computing.

Distributed Database: A database that, although forming an integral structure, is split into several segments for operational reasons.

Distributed Data Processing: Where data processing capabilities of an organisation are dispersed throughout the state or country. Often a feature of computer usage in large organisations.

Distributed server: Peer-to-peer network architecture, in which server functions are shared among the peer computers in the network and disk drives, printers, and other devices are available to all.

Distribution: The geographic range that a Usenet post is distributed to. By default, most newsreaders will give posts World distribution.

Distribution list: A simple form of mailing list in which an alias is assigned to a list of e-mail addresses. Mail directed to the alias is sent to every address on the list.

Disusered: (adj) Denied access to the Net, having an account cancelled.

DIX: *Digital, Intel and Xerox,* together the developers of the Ethernet protocol.

Documentation: This is the developer/manufacturer supplied information on how to use hardware and/or software. Documentation also refers to the commentary embedded into a computer program and to on-screen information, menus, error messages etc. Thorough documentation is the sign of a professional.

Dogpile: (v) To quickly follow up a Usenet post with a large volume of critical replies.

Domain: The main subdivision of Internet addresses, the last part of an Internet address after the final dot.

Domain name: A complete description of an Internet site including a host name, subdomain, and domain, all separated by dots.

Domain name address: An Internet address expressed in terms of host, subdomain, and domain, as opposed to the numerical IP address.

Domain name resolution: The process of converting domain names to numerical IP addresses, by consulting domain name servers.

Domain name server: An application that maintains a table of domain names and corresponding IP addresses in order to resolve the domain names of messages.

Domain Name System (DNS): A collection of distributed databases (domain name servers) that maintain the correlations between domain name addresses and numerical IP addresses, for example, the domain name address ruby.ora.com gets resolved into the numeric Internet address 134.65.87.3, and vice versa. DNS allows human beings to use the Internet with remembering long lists of numbers.

d00dz: B1FFspeak for *dudes,* a term of address.

DOS: *Disk Operating System,* the operating system developed for IBM PCs.

Dos2unix: A UNIX program that converts DOS text files to UNIX format (by stripping the carriage return character from the end of each line).

Dot: The separator character for domain names, newsgroup names, and other UNIX-oriented files. Dots should only be used to separate hierarchical levels in newsgroup names, not to split compound names.

Dot address: A 32-bit numerical IP address of the form *number-dot-number-dot-number-dot-number (such* as 192.100.81.101). Each of the four numbers can range from 0 to 255.

Dot file: A UNIX file whose name begins with a dot, such as profile, .netrc, .cshrc, and so on. Dot files will not show up in a normal directory listing.

Dot Matrix Printer: A generic name given to any printer that produces text (images) by combinations of dots. Most PC printers are dot matrix printers of one sort or another. A Laser Printer is essentially a dot matrix printer, however the term dot matrix is usually reserved for impact printers, where images are produced by the impact of different combinations of print pins. The resolution offered by a dot matrix printer can be gauged from the number of pins in the print head. Printers are advertised as being, for example, 9pin, 24pin, 32pin etc, the more pins the better the printed image.

Dots per Inch: A measure of print resolution which refers to the number of dots per linear inch that make up a character. Only applicable to those printers that use a matrix of dots to create characters, for example, Dot Matrix Printer, Laser Printer, Thermal Printer. Abbreviation dpi.

Double Density: On a "double density" floppy disk, the amount (areal density) of magnetic coating is twice that of a single density coating. This increases the memory capacity of the disk. The number of usable sides on a disk will also, affect capacity. A single sided 5.25' disk may have 160KB capacity, a double sided double density (abbreviation DSDD) may have 360KB and double sided high density (abbreviation DSHD) disk 1.2MB.

Doubled sig: A sig block that appears twice at the end the of an e-mail message or Usenet post, a sign that the writer is a newbie or that the software is hiccupping.

Double Precision Number: In some programming languages, this is an alternative name for floating point numbers. See Floating Point Number.

Down: (adj) Said of a network or device that is not functioning.

Downloading: The process of passing (loading) data from a large computer system to a smaller one. For example, from a mainframe to a PC. Downloading is also used to describe the process of passing information from a PC to a peripheral device, for example a Laser Printer. Soft fonts may be downloaded from a PC to a printer, hence the phrase "downloadable soft fonts". Increasingly the phrase downloading is not related to the relevant size of the computers involved. Any process of passing data from one computer to another can be referred to as downloading, the data source is said to be downloading the data. Uploading of downloading.

Downstream: Where your newsfeed goes after it has reached your host and your host a DUA has sent it along to other sites.

Down-Time: The period of time during which a computer is out of action. See also Mean Time Between Failure, Up-and-Running.

Downward Compatibility: This describes hardware or software that is compatible with previous versions of the same item. For example Z-Base 5 may be able to read Z-Base 4 files, in which case Z-Base 5 is downward compatible. Conversely Z-Base 1 may not be able to read Z-Base 5 files, in which case Z-Base 1 flies do not have upward compatibility. In any case the use of the phrases "downward" and upward" often depends on the user's reference point.

Draft: A preliminary copy of a finished document. Several be produced before the document is copies may used. Many printers have low and high resolution settings on thei · control panels. In low resolution settings the print characters are not precisely formed, however for a draft copy this is usually acceptable. High resolution settings are often labelled NLQ an abbreviation for 'Wear Letter Quality".

Drag: To move an on-screen object (usually graphics) from one part of the screen to another. Dragging is a feature offered by most PC graphics packages.

DRAM: Abbreviation for Dynamic Random Access Memory. This is computer memory (RAM) that loses its memory capability once the power source is removed. Most computer RAM is in fact DRAM, however it is usually described as being RAM.

Driver: Software that controls peripheral devices, such as monitors, printers, or keyboards.

Drive A: The first floppy disk drive on an IBM or IBM compatible PC. In the case of two drives, the A drive is usually the drive on the left or the top.

Drive B: The second floppy disk drive on an IBM or IBM compatible PC. The first drive (the A drive) is usually the leftmost or topmost drive. The B drive is usually the drive on the right or the bottom.

Drive C: The first logical hard disk drive on an IBM or IBM compatible PC.

Drive D: Drive Z. The logical hard disk drives on an IBM or IBM compatible PC.

Drop-Down Menu: This is a menu that does not have a fixed on-screen display, a drop-down menu only appears when a higher level menu is activated. Drop-down menus are also known as pop-up menus.

Drop-outs: Characters that are missing from the screen or not passed on by the keyboard.

DS4: *Digital Signal Level 4 is 274.176* Mbps, a standard level of digital transmission service.

DS1: *Digital Signal Level 1 is 1.544* Mbps, a standard level of digital transmission service.

DS3: *Digital Signal Level 3 is 44.7,36* Mbps, a standard level of digital transmission service.

DS2: *Digital Signal Level 2 is 6.312* Mbps, a standard level of digital transmission service.

DSO: *Digital Signal Level 0 is 64* Kbps, a standard level of digital transmission service.

Dumb terminal: A keyboard-and-monitor device that sends keystrokes to a computer and displays output on the screen. If you dial up to a UNIX shell, then your PC is being used as a dumb terminal.

Dummy variable: A meaningless variable used in an example to demonstrate correct syntax, such as foo, bar, or baz.

Dup killer: *(doop killer)* FidoNet software that tries to detect and eliminate duplicate copies 0', the same message that may have arrived via different routes.

E

Echo: (n) 1. A discussion group on FidoNet; 2. The, method by which the characters you type ire displayed on your screen, also know as local echo; 3. The method by which characters sent from a remote system are displayed on your screen.

EcoNet: A BBS dedicated to environmental issues. Its Internet domain name is igc.org.

EDGAR: *Electronic Data Gathering Archiving and Retrieval,* a database of corporate disclosure, transaction, and financial status data maintained by the United States Security Exchange Commission.

EDIFACT: Abbreviation for Electronic Data Interchange For Administration, Commerce and Transport.

EISA: Abbreviation for Extended Industry Standard Architecture. This is a bus architecture standard for personal computers proposed by a number of computer manufacturers and software developers.

Editing: The process of reviewing, and if necessary, changing the content and/or format of a document, spreadsheet etc.

Editor: 1. A text editor, a program used to edit simple text files; 2. Any program used to edit any type of file, such as a .WAV (Windows sound file) editor.

EDLIS: *Exchange of Dylan Lyrics—Internet Service,* an underground organization whose respond to requests posted in rec.music.dylan and elsewhere on the Net.

EDT: A text editor available on VMS machines and at Delphi Information Service.

.edu: The Internet domain dedicated to educational institutions.

EDUCOM: *(ed-you-com)* An *organization* dedicated to facilitating the use of computers in educational institutions. It is a supporter of the National Research and Education Network (NREN).

EFFs Guide to the Internet: Formerly Big *Dummy's Guide to the Electronic Frontier* Foundation's excellent free Internet guide, available via FTP, gopher, and the Web.

EIA/TIA-568: A document coauthored by the American National Standards Institute, the Electronics Industry Association, and the Telecommunications Industry Association that specifies a wiring standard for buildings suitable for both LANs and telecommunicationssystems.

E-journal: An *electronic journal,* an academic journal that circulates via an e-mail mailing list. One advantage-journals have over Print journals is that they are searchable.

Electronic Data Interchange: A national standard which specifies the protocol and format for the interchange of commercial documents. Abbreviation EDI.

Electronically Erasable Programmable Read Only Memory: A type of read only memory (ROM) that can be programmed (or reprogrammed) by electronic means. Electronically Erasable Programmable Read Only Memory is used in many electronic devices, not just computers.

Electronic Frontier Foundation: A lobbying and advocacy organization, founded by Mitch Kapor and John Barlow, working for the preservation of freedom on the cyberspace frontier.

Electronic Funds Transfer: Financial transaction processing via data communications links, abbreviation EFT.

Electronic Funds Transfer-Point of Sale: Financial transaction processing via data communications links. Examples include super-market check-outs, service stations etc.

Electronic journal: An academic journal that circulates via an e-mail mailing list.

Electronic Mail: Any information that is transmitted via a computer system or communications network. Abbreviation e-Mail or E-Mail.

Electronic Office: A generic term for a hi-tech office that uses many electronic business machines such as computers, modems, fax, photocopiers, cordless telephones etc.

Electronics Industries Association (EIA): A standards organization for the electronics industry, the coauthor of ElA/TIA-568.

Electronic White Pages: A service provided by Telecom Australia which enables computer users to access the white pages telephone directory via a data communications network.

Elm: (rhymes with *helm)* A full-screen UNIX e-mail program, easier to use than the basic, line-at-a-time mail but still more difficult than pine, which is much closer to modern word processors.

Emacs: A UNIX text editor that doubles as an operating environment, mail program, and newsreader.

E-mail: (n) Short for *electronic mail,* one of the most popular features of networks, online services, and the Internet in general, but you already knew that, didn't you? The term *e-mail is* used both for the overall process and for the messages carried electronically from computer to computer.

E-mail address: 1. An Internet mail address of the form *username@host.domain;* 2. The username portion of a mail account on a network.

e me: Send me e-mail, please reply by e-mail.

Emulation: To copy the characteristics of a particular hard-ware device. For example, the ABCD Laser Printer has three emulations, the VFG 200, the YUK 90 and the ARG 50, meaning that the ABCD can be treated as being "identical" in most aspects to the other printers in terms of printer drivers.

Encapsulate: To embed a higher-level protocol within a lower-level protocol to create a single frame for trans-portation over a network

Encapsulated PostScript (EPS): A device-independent file format for PostScript files. EPS files are portable and can be printed with any PostScript printer.

Encoding: The process of converting data to a coded for-mat, generally to make it more easily transportable.

Encrypt: To scramble the contents of a file or e-mail mes-sage so that only those with the key can unscramble and read them.

Encryption: A coding technique used to provide security for data being transmitted over a communications channel. The data is encrypted into an agreed format by the sender and restored to its original format at the receiving end.

Encryption key: A unique, secret data block used to encrypt e-mail.

End-to-end: (adj) Direct, said of a connection between two computers.

End-user: (n) From a programmer's perspective, the ultimate customer, the regular person using the program, operating system, or computer.

Enter key: A large key on the right side of most keyboards used to submit commands or insert hard returns into text.

Enterprise computing: Corporate network computing, bridging a variety of platforms, operating systems, and networking protocols.

Enterzone: A hyperzine on the World Wide Web at http:// enterzone.berkeley,

Environment: A front end for an operating system, a set of tools and a consistent look and feel that allow the user to interact with the computer. Windows is an environment that runs on top of die MS-DOS operating system.

End-of-File: A phrase used in many programming languages to indicate that processes are complete. A character used to denote that the end of a file has been reached. *The* end-of-file marker is often a Control-Z (^Z), a particular combination of binary digits which is recognised by the program control.

End-User: In Systems Analysis, this is the final user of the computer system. For example, a Systems Analyst may discuss computer software with a software developer and talk of the "enduser's requirements".

ENIAC: Abbreviation for Electronic Numerical Integrator and Calculator. One of the first computers of the First Generation, developed in the USA during the early 1940s. ENIAC used vacuum tubes and had a MTBF of about two hours.

ENTER Key: The key used to signal that keyboard input is ready for processing. Typically the ENTER key is pressed after each command. In some documentation the ENTER key is designated RETURN. Pressing the ENTER key empties the keyboard buffer.

Ergonomics: The study of the Workplace and furniture design in relation to work processes. The key aim of ergonomics is to improve health, safety, and efficiency in the workplace. Recent studies in ergonomics have also investigated the impact of colour in the workplace, not only the colour of office furniture, walls etc, but the colours used on computer monitors. It has been found that a monochrome monitor using green is the least tiring to the eyes whereas amber produces the least number of operator mistakes.

Eris: The Goddess of Discord.worshipped by members of the Discordian Society.

Error: An unexpected action or result, or incorrectly transmitted data. Any process that causes results which a computer cannot properly interpret.

Error control: Any method for verifying the correctness of transmitted data.

Error Message: A message generated by a software application or hardware device in response to a hardware, software or user error.

Error Rate: This is the number of errors that occur during data transmission.

Escape character: 1. ASCII 26; 2. Any character which, when preceded by an escape, sends a command to a device, such as a terminal or printer.

Escape Key: This is a key found on many computer keyboards which is used to start an "escape" sequence. This may be backtracking out of a menu or activating a menu etc.

Escape out: (v) 1. To substitute a special symbol for a character that would otherwise be misinterpreted; 2. To run a temporary shell from within an application in order to send commands to the operating system.

Escape Sequence: A series of command codes sent to a peripheral device to instruct the printer to perform a particular task, such as change the font for the next character, to indent the text, change the line spacing etc. Different printer command languages have their own codes, as do different printers. Escape codes are embedded into the data being sent from the computer and are invariably usertransparent.

Ethernet: A Local Area Network (LAN) implementation protocol developed by Xerox Corporation, Digital Equipment Corporation and Intel. Ethernet is one of the most popular LAN implementations and several industry standards are based on it.

EtherTalk: AppleTalk protocols for Ethernet LANs, encapsulating DDP datagrams into Ethernet frames.

EtherTalk Link Access Protocol (ELAP): AppleTalk's Ethernet data link protocol.

ETLA: *(ee-tee-ell-ay) Extended three-letter acrony.* The acronym is a facetious comment on the proliferation of bewildering TLAs in the technical world. Too many TLAs and ETLAs thrown around make MEGO.

Eudora: An e-mail program for Windows or the Macintosh that can use the Post Office Protocol and function as an offline mail reader. Available via anonymous FTP from ftp.qualcomm.com.

European Academic and Research Network (EARN): A network of universities and research facilities in Europe that has e-mail and file-transfer connections to BITNET.

Even parity: A method of verifying the correctness of transmitted data by summing each byte, adding a parity bit of 1 if necessary to ask the sum even before sending the data, and then repeating the summation on the receiving end.

Exclamation point: (!) 1. A bang—it precedes each site in a bang path; 2. In some UNIX programs, an exclamation mark enables the user to shell out; 3. Overuse of exclamation marks to punctuate Usenet posts is one of the hallmarks of a newbie or a BIFF.

.exe: A DOS file extension used to indicate an executable file (such as a program or self-extracting archive file).

Execute: To perform a command or run a program, something operating systems do.

Executable File: This is computer software that contains instructions for the CPU and computer peripherals. Executable files can be "run", that is they produce tangible events via the CPU instruction set. Conversely, data files are passive and are only useful in conjunction with an executable file.

Exit: (v) To quit a program or leave a shell.

Expanded Memory: On an IBM and IBM compatible PC, this is memory that is accessible via a 16KB "window" within the first 1MB of RAM.

Expansion Slot: These are slots (electrical connectors) on a motherboard reserved for the addition of more RAM, extra peripherals etc.

Expert System: A specialised computer system, usually dealing with a narrow range of expertise, for example, land management, scientific analysis.

Expire: Applied to Usenet articles, to be removed after an expiration date to keep the newsfeed from growing too large.

Export: (v) 1. To save a file in a different format; 2. To send a product to a foreign country.

Extended Binary Coded Decimal Interchange Code (EBCDIC): A proprietary IBM character set that is not entirely compatible with ASCII.

Extended Memory: On an IBM and IBM compatible PC, this is memory above the first 1MB boundary, that is above "conventional" memory.

Extension: This usually refers to the second part of a file name. Operating systems allow a certain number of characters for the file name and an additional group of characters as a file extension.

External command: In MS-DOS this is a command that is not available via the generic command processor and requires the loading of an executable file.

External Disk Drive: A disk drive whose hardware is physically separate to the computer hardware. Electrically it will perform the same function as an internal drive.

External Gateway Protocol (EGP): A routing protocol by which connected net works signal their availability to each other.

External schema: A database subschema that pertains to the scope of a particular user's view of the database.

F

Fabrication: The processing of manufacturing materials to described specifications.

Facsimile: A data communications device that can transmit images via ordinary telephone circuits. At the transmitting end a document is fed into the facsimile machine (also known as a fax machine or simply fax) which then scans and digitises the document.

Fair use: The legal doctrine that allows limited quotation of other people's work if the use of their work does not undercut its market value.

Fall off: Said of a portion of data that exceeds the size of a memory register and is lost.

Fanzine: An underground, do-it-yourself magazine, often dedicated to a band, celebrity, or cult figure.

FAQ: (fack,n) 1. *frequently asked question*; 2. A file containing frequently asked questions and their answers, sometimes called a FAQL (*frequently asked question list*). To find FAQs, look in the answers newsgroups or the FTP archive at rtfm.mit.edu. Many mailing lists and Usenet newsgroups maintain FAQs so that participants won't have to spend lots of time answering the same set of questions.

FAQL: (*fackle,* n) *Frequently asked question list,* a file cont-aining frequently asked questions and their answers, usually compiled and maintained by a newsgroup, mailing list, or Internet site.

FARNET (Federation of American Research Networks): A nonprofit organization that works to promote the use of computer networks for research and education.

FAST: Abbreviation for Federation Against Soft-ware Theft. An

American software industry association with obvious objectives.

Fast packet: A standard for highspeed, hightraffic, cellswitching networks.

Fax: 1. A *facsimile* of a document, digitized and transmitted over phone lines. While faxes are usually sent and received with a standalone fax machine, faxes may also be sent to and from computers using fax software and a fax modem; 2. A machine that can send and receive faxes.

Fax modem: A modem that can fulfill some of the functions of a fax machine.

FCC: Abbreviation for Federal Communications Commission, an American statutory body, concerned with many aspects of communications. For example, the FCC issues Class A and Class B certificates, relating to suppression of radio interference (RE). Class A certificates cover usage in commercial premises, whilst the more stringent Class B certificate covers residential usage. Most countries have an equivalent system of certification.

FDC: Abbreviation for Floppy Disk Controller.

FDD: 1) Floppy Disk Drive. 2) Fixed Disk Drive. Another name for Hard Disk Drive.

Federal Information Exchange (FIX): A gateway linking U.S. government net works with the Internet.

Federal Information Processing Standards (FIPS): A United States Department of Defense document specifying U.S. government networking plans.

Federal Networking Council (FNC): An organization that coordinates the net working standards of U.S. government agencies.

FEDIX: An online information service linking educational institutions and the U.S. government.

Fetch: A step in a machine cycle where the next instruction or batch of required data is retrieved from RAM or secondary memory.

Fiber Distributed Data Interface (FDDI): A backbone, system for large networks, employing two rings of fiberoptic cabling, with a signaling rate of 80 Mbps.

Fibre Optics: A data communications method that uses glass fibres to channel light through a cable. Given the high frequency of light this provides a very powerful trans-mission media, with many thousands of connections per fibre being possible.

Fiberoptic cable: Class cabling designed to carry light pulses, often used for backbones; more dependable, lighter, and smaller than copper cable carrying electronic signals, but much more expensive and more difficult to repair.

FidoNet: A network of BBSs with Internet email access.

Field: This is a data entry area in a database, with each field being specified by a label, a size and a data type.

56K: Said of a telephone circuit with a 64 Kbps bandwidth that uses 8K for signaling and the remaining 56K for traffic.

First in -First out (FIFO): A design philosophy employed in queueing, gating and spooling systems. This philosophy ensures that waiting times are roughly equally for all users.

Fight-o-net: A pejorative name for FidoNet, alluding to the frequent arguments on FidoNet echoes and mailing lists.

File: A collection of data items, text or numerical information created by computer software during the exe-cution of a program. Files are normally stored on tape or disk. A word processing file may contain, for example, a quotation for a job, a chapter of a book, an annual report or a memo. A database file may contain a listing of names, addresses, postcodes, telephone numbers and employee numbers. A spreadsheet file may contain financial data for the present financial year.

File Allocation Table: A data file, on a floppy disk or hard disk, detailing the location of each file that has been written on to the disk. This enables the operating system to locate and read or update each file whenever necessary. The File Allocation Table (abbreviation FAT) is stored in duplicate because of the possibility of bad sectors making the FAT unreadable and the disk therefore useless.

File Attach: A FidoNet procedure for attaching a file to an email message to send it to another BBS.

File locking: Preventing all but the first user from changes to a file that is opened by more than one user on a network.

File Name: The name given to a data file, system file or executable file. In many cases the file name must be given by the computer user before the computer can write the file to disk or tape. When a software application makes a request for access to a particular file, the operating system converts the file name to a storage address ready for retrieval. Most operating systems restrict the file name length to a maximum number of characters (for example, under MS-DOS this is eight characters). It is useful to make a file name indicative of the file contents. For example a word processing file called XYZ-AP8.doc might be a letter sent to X= P/L on April 8th. FIN89-90.WKI might be a company's financial records spreadsheet for the financial year 1989-90.

File Protection Ring: A small plastic ring on a reel-to-reel tape that is used to "write-protect" the tape.

File request: A FidoNet procedure for transferring a file from one BBS to another.

File Server: A microprocessor controlled device that controls the flow of data to and from terminals in a Local Area Network. A File Server 'serves' software and data to each terminal.

File transfer: The copying of a file over a network connection from a remote site to the localhost.

Fill-in Screen: A data entry screen that provides a number of boxes and lines as data entry points. Each data entry point is presented in a logical order and has an appropriate label to indicate which data item should go where. This type of screen is often used for airline reservations and similar systems and is also known as a Data Entry Screen.

Film at 11: A common tag line in Usenet follow-up posts mocking the timeliness of the original article. Often follows "Imminent death of the Net predicted!"

Filter: A software command that either extracts data items from a database in a particular order and/or extracts only certain data items from the database. The first case is sometimes referred to as indexing, the second case as querying.

Finder: A part of the operating system on an Apple com-puter, which provides file and directory management facilities.

Finger: To seek the identity of a user or the status of a net-work. The UNIX command that performs the finger function.

Finn: To pull rank on someone else in IRC by showing that you've been around a lot longer than the other person—a relative newbie compared to you.

Firewall: A security measure on the Internet, protecting information, preventing access, or ensuring that users cannot do any harm to underlying systems. Some networks are connected to the Internet via a firewall machine.

Firmware: This term is used to describe the software embedded into ROM (read-only-memory). This software is usually written into ROM during manufacture and cannot subsequently be changed by programmers or users. Firmware provides basic control routines for the CPU and computer hardware.

First Generation Computer: These were computers dev-eloped between about 1940-1960, First Generation Computers used vacuum tube technology and consumed awesome amounts of power and floor space.

FirstSearch Catalog: A catalog maintained by the Online Computer Library Center that gives member libraries access to many databases of books and magazines in print.

Fixed Length Record: A data record that has a fixed amount of space reserved for it regardless of whether that space will be used or not. For example, in a database it may be necessary to reserve up to 30 characters for a person's surname, but in practice most surnames would fall far short of this size. In large databases (such as a payroll database for a large organisation) fixed length records can mean an enormous amount of wasted data storage capability.

Fixed Space Font: A design of font that allocates the same linear space to each printed character. By comparison a Proportionally Spaced Font allocates variable linear space to different characters. For example, using proportional spacing, the letter 'w' would be given more space than the letter "i". Use of proportional spacing gives a much more professional appearance to text. Most word processors can specify proportional spacing (proportionally spaced fonts) but not all printers can produce 'the necessary output.

Flag: A register that stores the status of a device (microprocessor, hardware etc).

Flame: An insulting e-mail or Usenet post. Flames are often illconsidered kneejerk expressions of anger, but they can also be cruelly detailed and intended for the amusement of the general audience at the expense of the flamee.

Flamebait: A post to a mailing list or newsgroup designed to elicit flames.

Flamebait: can be recognized by the fact that it goes beyond the premises of the list or newsgroup. No-body objects to provocative or even argumentative posts, but posts to the alt.fank.frank-zappa newsgroup saying "Zappa was a no-talent potty-mouthed dweeb" betray a lack of legitimate interest in the subject hand.

Flamefest: A flame war, particularly one involving many participants.

Flame on A comment in a post meaning either "Here is where I start flaming" or "I'm prepared to be flamed for the following comment."

Flamer: 1. One who flames; 2. One who flames habitually or incessantly.

Flames to /dev/null: A tag line in posts to mailing lists and newsgroups meaning "I'll ignore any flames", from the UNIX name for the null device, a sort of trash can.

Flame war: Often written *flamewar,* a prolonged series of flames and counter-flames, drowning out the on-topic posts in a newsgroup or mailing list. Traditionally, flame wars end when Nazis are mentioned.

Flavor: (n) A variety, as in "BSD is a flavor of UNIX"

Flip-Flop: A part of the internal circuitry of a register. It recognises and responds to binary input, the circuitry of the register "flips" and "flops" between two states (0 and 1). In combinations it is used as a logic gate, as well as a shift register.

Floating Point Numbers: These are numbers that can be represented by a variable amount of decimal places. Decimal representation can be achieved in binary numbering by allocating certain positions as "decimals". For example, in a 16-bit word, 12 bits can be allocated to be the actual number and the remaining 4 bits to represent the decimal places.

The normal method of storing numbers is referred to a "fixed point" numbers, that is the decimal point is not moved throughout any computer operation, either for data storage or for processing. This creates problems when dealing with large numbers and "floating point" notation is used. For example, the number 13678123410 can be represented by using floating point notation. In this system each large number is converted to a decimal and a, corresponding "power of ten" multiplier. In the example given, this could be 0. 1367812341 x 10 ^ 11 or 1367.7812341 x 10 ^ 7. In this manner the CPU is able to manipulate otherwise unwieldy numbers with accuracy.

In some programming languages (for example, C) program variables can be declared as being "floating point". Variables should only be declared as floating point if absolutely necessary as these numbers will have a large amount of RAM allocated to them.

Flood: (v) To spam an IRC channel, that is, to type or paste in huge amounts of text, effectively drowning out the conversation.

Floppy Disk: A magnetic storage media, using flat, circular platters. Floppy disks are primarily used on PCs. Physical size and storage capabilities vary. Some examples are,

Size capacity

5.25"160KB, 360KB, 1.2MB

3.5" 160KB, 360KB, 400KB, 720KB, 800KB, 1M, 1.44MB; 2.8MB

Floppy disks first came on the market in the early-1970s. The 5.25" (135mm) disk appeared to be the industry standard for many years but is now being challenged by the more robust, more compact, larger storage, 3.5" (90mm) disks. The even smaller 2" disk has yet to make its impact.

Floppy Disk Drive: An electro-mechanical device that performs read/write operations on a floppy disk. The disk drive has a read/write head which accesses and, if necessary, updates data files on disk. The disk drive rotates the internal magnetic media of the disk at about 360 revolutions per minute, ensuring that all areas of the disk appear under the read/write head at frequent intervals.

Floptical Disk: A type of floppy disk that combines optical and magnetic techniques. These disks have a very high density of data storage tracks and hence a high storage capacity. As this is a comparatively new technology, floptical disks have yet to make their impact.

Flow Chart: A graphical representation of the major steps in a computer program or the manufacturing/commercial processes involved in producing goods or services. Most flow charts are based upon a standard method of indicating the different types of processes that may be involved. The following is an example of a flow chart using ANSI symbols.

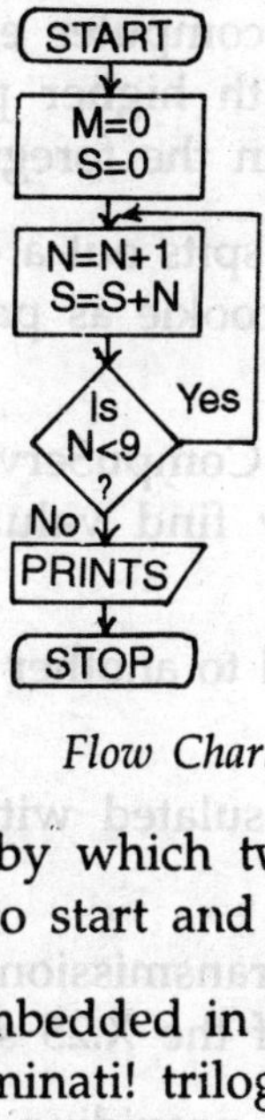

Flow Chart

Flow control: The method by which two devices, generally modems, signal to each other when to start and stop sending data.

fnord: A nonsense word embedded in posts or sig blocks, alluding to Robert Anton Wilson's Illuminati! trilogy.

FOAF: A *friend of a friend,* the most comon source or attribution for urban legends, implying that the teller doesn't personelly know the participants, but knows someone who does.

Folder: 1. A directory, especially on a Macintosh; 2. An e-mail file containing related messages.

Follow-up: To respond to a post with a replying post.

Follow-up: A post that replies to and possibly quotes an earlier post.

Follow-up line: A line in the header of some Usenet posts directing follow-ups to a particular newsgroup or newsgroups. Newbies who fail to heed the follow-up line can be tricked into posting replies to inappropriate newsgroups.

Foo: A dummy variable used by programmers as a stand-in for a real variable, often paired with bar.

Foobar: A dummy variable used by programmers as a stand-in for a real variable.

Footprint: The portion of a surface that the computer or other device occupies.

Foreground: In a multitasking computer environment, a process that takes place in full view or with higher prioriy than other running processes is said to take place in the foreground.

Fortune cookie: A program that spits out a different fortune every time you run it. Some systems run cookie as part of their startup or login procedure.

Forum: A discussion group on CompuServe and other online services and BBSs where interests may find valuable information exchange ideas and share files.

Forward: To send received e-mail to another address, either manually or automatically.

Frame: A block of data encapsulated with a header and trailer for transmission over a network.

Frame relay: A standard for transmission of frames over a packet-switching net-work, a variant of the X.25 standard.

Free-net: A free public network providing Internet access to members of a community.

Free Software Foundation (FSF): An organization dedicated to the production and distribution of the free software the creators of GNU, reachable via FTP at prep.ai.mit.edu.

Free-WAIS: A free version of a WAIS server produced and distributed, by CNIDR (Clearinghouse for Networked Information Discovery and Retrieval).

Freeware: Software distributed for free (or bragging rights) via the Net. The culture, of the Internet encourages freeware.

Frequency: A measurement of the number of cycles per second of an electronic signal, roughly a measurement of the speed of a process or device.

FSLIST: The Forgotten Site List. A list of Internet service providers available via anonymous FTP from freedom.nmsu.edu in the /pub/docs/fslist directory.

FTP: Internet *file transfer protocol,* the standard TCP/IP protocol for transferring files over the Internet, across any platforms.

G

G: Symbol for the word "Giga" (one thousand million) and in computer usage this is the quantity 1073741824 (2^30) not 1000000000 as in normal business and scientific usage.

Gantt Chart: An activity monitoring method commonly used in business. It is usually in the form of a bar chart, and shows actual progress against planned progress of an activity. Named after Henry Gantt (1861-1919) a management theorist and a writer of the scientific management school.

Gas Plasma Display: Ibis is a type of monitor display which is used in some portable computers. Gas plasma provides better definition than a Liquid Crystal Display, but at the price of higher power consumption. It uses inert gases, such as neon.

Gate: (n) Also called a gateway a computer providing a connection between two works, two e-mail handling systems, or a Usenet newsgroup and a mailing list.

Gated: (adj) Connected to another network or discussion group via a gateway.

Gated newsgroup: A news-group whose posts are sent to a mailing list and which receives (or includes) posts from the mailing list.

Gateway: Any link between two data communications networks.

Geek: Someone who knows a lot about computers, networks, or the Internet and thinks they're interesting (not necessarily an insult).

Geek code: A set of coded ratings in a sig block. describing the poster in humorous, geeky terms.

Gender Bender: A small electrical connector that inverts the gender of an electrical connector (male > female, female-> male).

General Public License (GPL): Also called copyleft, the license carried by Free Software Foundation software, granting reuse and reproduction rights to anyone and everyone.

General Public Virus (GPV): A pejorative name for the General Public License carried by Free Software Foundation software, so called because some developers believe it opens them up to legal liability if they include GPL code in their products.

Generation (computers): Evolutionary steps in technological progress are often referred to as being "of the next generation". The actual boundary between one generation and another is hard to define, but the concept of successive generations remains.

In computers it is acknowledged that First Generation was from 1940-1960, using vacuum tube technology; Second Generation from approximately 1955-1965, using transistor technology, but only as discrete components; Third Generation from approximately 1965-1980, using low density integrated circuits and microprocessors; Fourth Generation from approximately 1980, using Very Large Scale Integration (VLSI).

Generation (languages): In computer programming the present crop of formal, structured, syntax dependent languages are Third Generation (also known as 3GL). Examples include BASIC, PASCAL and C. The newer, less .formal languages, for example, DataFlex, are known as Fourth Generation languages.

Geographic information system: A computer system, both hardware and software, which is used to analyse geographic information, for example, the distribution of natural resources, land usage patterns, demographic trends etc. A Geographic Information System (abbreviation GIS) is not necessarily an on-line system. It usually draws data from external primary and secondary sources. Its tasks may include cartography, time-series analysis, statistics and databases.

Get: (v) To copy a file from a remote source to your host computer, particularly via FIT. (n) The FTP command to get a file.

Get a life: A common flame, suggesting that the flame is too involved in the Internet or her/his computer.

Get a real: A common geeky type of flame directed at someone's inferior hardware, software, or network connection.

Ghod: An alternative spelling for God preferred by some hackers and other netizens/also spelled *ghod).*

Ghu: A deity some hackers and other netizens offer their praises and curses to, as in "Great Ghu! Where'd you get an idea like that?"

GIF (Graphics Interchange Format): 1. An extremely popular compressed graphics (image) file format originated by *CompuServe* but readable in most platforms; 2. A file in the GIF format.

GIF! GIF! GIF!: A ritual followup to a post mentioning an image (such as a photograph), requesting that someone scan the image, save it as a GIF, uuencode it, and post it to the newsgroup.

Gigabyte: A measure of secondary memory capacity. One gigabyte (abbreviation GB) is 1024 Megabytes. Secondary memory on a mainframe computer is typically measured in GB.

GIGO: Abbreviation for Garbage in Garbage out. A reminder that the finished product is only as good as the raw materials, hardware, software, data and personnel involved in a project.

Glitch: Computer jargon for a program failure or human mistake.

Global: Affecting an entire document or system (for example, a global search and replace is a search and replace operation performed on an entire document than a small selection or a single item)

Global variable: A variable whose value is controlled by any part of the program. A global variable is accessible to the main program and other modules, any of which may be able to alter its value.

Glossary: A listing of definitions, usually found at the back of the more professional computing books.

GNU: (noo) A freely distributed set of applications and utilities intended as replacement for UNIX GNU is distributed by the Free Software Foundation.

Godwin's Rule: Usenet Rule #4, which states that a thread in which Nazis or Hitler have been invoked has reached irrelevancy and will end soon. For some (but not all) of the other Rules see the net.legends FAQ at gopher://dixie. aiss.uinc.edu: 6969/00/urban.legends/ net.legends/Net.Legends.FAQ.

Good Thing: Something generally or widely accepted to be good. Tolerance is a Good thing. so is reading the FAQ before asking questions.

Gopher: A client/server application that allows you to browse huge amounts of information by performing FTP transfers, remote logins, archie searches, and on, presenting everything to the end-user in the form of menus. This saves the user from having to know (or type in) the address of the Internet resources being tapped.

Gopher Book for Windows: A gopher client for Windows, available via anonymous FTP from sunsite.unc.edu.

Gopher client: The gopher program that an end-user runs to get information from a gopher server. The gopher client retrieves the menus and documents and displays them for the user.

Gopher.micro.umn.edu: The site of the University of Minnesota Gopher, the original gopher server.

Gopher for Nextstep: A gopher client for the Nextstep operating system, available via anonymous FTP from sonata.cc. purdue.edu.

Gopher server: An application that provides documents and menus to gopher client, a starting point for a gopher search.

Gopher site: A computer with a gopher server running on it.

Gopherspace: A conceptual space encompassing all of the menus and documents that can be reached via the interconnected system of gopher serves on the Internet.

Gorets: (n) A generic noun that can have any meaning, especially as elaborated in the alt.gorets, especially as elaborated in the alt.gorets newsgroup.

Go root: (v) To log in as root, a UNIX superuser or system administrator account, in order to exercise the extended privileges of that account.

GOTO: A program statement used in several high-level programming languages, for example, BASIC, PASCAL, C. GOTO statements transfer program control to another line of code and may be conditional or unconditional.

.gov: An Internet domain corresponding to U.S government, including federal , state, and logical governments.

Government OSI Profile (GOSIP): A set of OSI standards that the U.S government follows in the procurement of computers in order to preserve compatibility among various government computer networks.

Grape juice: Something you yell at a computer when it isn't working, akin to banging it on the side.

Graph: Any pictorial representation of business or statistical information, often called charts, rather than graphs. Many PC software applications provide graphics capabilities, for example, SYSTAT, Excel, Lotus 123, Quattro, SPSS etc.

Graphical user interface (GUI): A fullscreen graphical Interface (meaning not limited to just letters and numbers) that allows users to run programs, execute commands, and generally interact with the computer by using a pointing device such as mouse to manipulate graphical screen elements, as opposed to typing commands at a prompt.

Dial-up Internet users generally need SLIP or PPP access to be able to interact direclty with Internet facilities within their GUI.

<gr&d>: (written only) Grinning running and ducking (what you post after you've tweaked someone). Also <gd&r>.

Graphics program: Software that can be used to generate general purpose drawings or specific industry drawings, for example, engineering, cartography, business etc.

Great renaming: A day in 1985 on which nonlocal Usenet newsgroup names were changed from the form net.* to the hierarchy still in use today.

Great worm: The 1988 worm that got out of control and crashed systems all over the internet. throwing a scare into many.

Greeking: The use of symbols to show text or graphics that cannot be shown in sufficient detail to be legible. For example a very small font may be shown on the monitor as xxxxx.

Green-card lawyer: A pejorative term for people who *spam* the Net with unwanted advertisements and then go on TV to defend their actions.

Group: (n) Generally, a news group, a Usenet or similar style discussion group.

Groupware: Software that gives multiple users access to the same information over a network, allowing collaboration on documents, scheduling of meetings, tracking of mission-critical projects, and so on.

H

^H: The backspace character. Use of the Backspace key in terminal emulations chat don't support it sometimes leaves the original text on-screen, followed by one ^H character for every time. Backspace is pressed, as in "Let me be the first to call you a H^H^H^H friend."

Hack: To write code, to work on a computer, to cleverly diagnose and fix a problem, to dig beneath the surface of a computer process, reinventing things when hack around.

Hacker: A computer adept, someone who enjoys working with computer, and testing the limits of systems, an enthusiastic or fast (or both) programmer.

Hacker ethic: The philosophy, common among hackers, that information, technology, and clever tricks should be shared and disseminated rather than hoarded.

Half bridge: A device that connects a network to a communications link via a modem without passing routing information, which must be supplied by the network software

Half duplex: Two-way communication in which the computers at each end of the transmission take turns sending.

Half router: A device that connects a network to a communications link via a modem, passing routing information along with data.

Handle: A nickname or one-word name, such as a nick on IRC or a user-name.

Handshake: Protocol for a data communications or data transfer circuit, for example, agreement on Baud Rate, Parity etc. Engineers may talk of "handshaking problems".

Hands-on: This refers to situations where a person actually uses computer hardware/software. Often called "hands-on experience". A computer operator may write in a job application "Five years hands-on experience, IBM 370. In an educational/training situation the syllabus may say "One hour lecture, followed by three hours hands-on".

Hang: Said of a computer, to, stop working, to freeze, to become unresponsive, to wait for something that will never happen.

Hard Card: In a PC, this is secondary memory in the form of a plug-in card which includes a hard disk.

Hard Copy: A generic term used to describe any form of computer output that produces a permanent record, for example, on paper, transparency, microfiche etc.

Hard Disk: A magnetic storage media, using flat, circular platters which are rotated at very high speed, typically 3600 revolutions per minute. The high speed of rotation ensures that all areas of the disk appear under the read/write heads at very frequent intervals. Physical size and storage capabilities vary. For PCs, sizes vary from 20MB to about 200MB. On mainframe computers, sizes vary from 500MB to several GB. Hard disks have been in use since the mid-1950s, when IBM introduced their "Ramac" hard disk.

Hard Disk Controller: Electronic circuitry that provides an interface to, and supeivises, a hard disk drive. Abbreviation HDC. There are several different controller philosophies in use, for example, ESDI, MFM, SCSI, ST506.

Hard Disk Drive: An electromechanical device that performs read/write operations to a hard disk. The disk drive has at least one read/write head which accesses and, if necessary, updates data files on disk. The disk drive rotates the platter(s) of the disk at about 3600 revolutions per minute, ensuring that all areas of the disk appear under the read/write head at very frequent intervals. Abbreviation HDD.

Hard Space: In word processing this is a space that is important for the meaning of the text. For example it may be considered bad style to allow word wrap to split the name "Ms Bingham!" over two lines. The insertion of a "hard" space between the two words will ensure that white space appears between the two words but that the words are treated as one.

Hardware: A generic term used for all of the electronic and electromechanical devices associated with a computer. This includes the computer cabinet itself, disk and tape drives, monitors, mice etc.

Hardware address: A specific physical address assigned to a device.

Hardware flow control: A form of flow control that is governed by devices themselves, instead of by communications software.

Hard Wiring: Fixed wiring that is a part of any computer or communications system. Once installed, hard wiring is rarely changed during the lifetime of the system.

Harris' Lament: "All the good ones are taken!"

Hash: A symbol (usually #) echoed at regular intervals to show that a process is still underway. The ftp command that causes the hash symbols to be displayed.

Hat: A common name for the caret character, ^ (ASCII 94), used to indicate exponents and to underscore text on the previous line in e-mail and Usenet posts.

Hayes-compatible: Said of a modem that understands the Hayes AT instruction set. Most modems today are Hayes- compatible.

HD: Abbreviation for High Density.

Head Cresh: A term used to describe the collision of a read/write head with a disk platter. Ibis is mostly a problem on hard disks as the separation of read/write head and platter is often less that 20 microns. A head crash can occur if the disk is subject to violent shock whilst in motion or if a foreign particle gets wedged under the head.

Header: The rows of information at the top of an e-mail message that include who the message is from, who it's to, when it was sent, and what it's about. Information preceding the data in a packet, specifying the addresses of the source and the destination as well as error-checking information.

Heap: Part of random access memory (RAM) set aside for usage during program execution.

Hello world: The output of most C programmers' first program, from Kernighan & Ritchie's canonical C text, The C programming Language.

Help: A command that will bring up help information in some programs and in some operating systems.

Help Menu: An on-screen display of user-friendly information, designed to help users of software applications to answer queries about the software without resorting to instruction manuals. Help

Menus are usually called up by pressing a single key or by making a selection from another menu. Many are context sensitive, this means, for example, that if the user wants help during the setting up of a style sheet, then the Help Menu would immediately provide information on this aspect of the package.

Hercules Card: A high resolution video (monitor) controller card. Commonly used for high resolution monochrome displays.

Hetboy: A heterosexual male, used most often in alt.sex groups.

Heterogeneous network: A network that includes various types of computers, operating systems, network cards, and so on, which therefore must be capable of different network protocols.

Hetgirl: A heterosexual female, used most often in alt.sex groups.

Hex: Abbreviation for Hexadecimal. Pertaining to a numerical system base 16. Hexadecimal digits are represented by the numerals 0 through 9 and the letters A through F. Because 16 is a multiple of 2, it is easy tom convert binary numbers into hexadecimal numbers, and some programs display data in hexadecimal form.

Hexadecimal Numbering: A numbering system that has 16 possible digits, 0-9 and A-F. Hexadecimal numbering is a convenient shorthand notation for binary numbering and is widely used in writing assembly language code and for addressing different parts of computer memory.

Arithmetic operations can be carried out using hexadecimals (and any other numbering system) so long as the rules of the particular system are adhered to.

Hiccup: Said of a network or applicamistakenly skip some data or send it more than once.

Hidden File: A file that is not normally displayed by a file listing, for example, the MS-DOS and VAX DIR command. Under MS-DOS the files IO.SYS and DOS.SYS are hidden files.

Hierarchical Database: A database in which the relationship of different data elements to one another is similar to the relationship of leaves on a tree to twigs, branches, large branches, the tree trunk itself and leaves, twigs etc on other branches.

Hierarchical file system: A system of arranging files in directories and subdirectories to maintain hierarchical relationships between the files and make them easier to find and retrieve.

Hierarchical routing: A system of routing in which different parts of a large network are arranged in a hierarchical tree and each level takes care of routing information to subordinate levels. The Internet maintains three different routing levels: backbone networks, midlevel networks, and stub networks.

Hierarchy: In file storage, the arrangement of directories into a tree of parents and children. In networks, the arrangement of levels for routing purposes. In Usenet, the organization of newsgroups into general areas, topics, and subtopics, or the major groupings themselves.

High Density: On a "high density" floppy disk, the amount (areal density) of magnetic coating is much greater than that of a single or double density coating. Ibis obviously increases the memory capacity of the disk. The number of usable sides on a disk will also affect capacity.

High-Level Data Link Control (HDLC): An ISO protocol for the data link layer of X.25 and OSI networks. It specifies that data is sent in frames that may vary in length.

High Level Language: A programming language that uses grammatical and mathematical notation reasonably similar to everyday language. Examples include BASIC, FORTRAN and PASCAL.

Highlighting: This is when a selection of on-screen text is differentiated from other text by means of keyboard commands or a mouse. The selected text is distinguished in some way, for example by a change in colour or the text may go to an enhanced display or inverse (reverse) video.

High Performance Parallel Interface (HPPI): An ANSI standard for connecting supercomputers to other devices, such as routers and other computers.

High Resolution: A measure of the precision of computer output, hard copy and soft copy. In the case of hard copy printed characters, high resolution implies an output of at least 240dpi. In the case of soft copy (monitor display) about 1000 x 850 pixels. High resolution monitors are kind to the eyes and less fatiguing to work in front of than low resolution monitors.

HIPO Chart: Abbreviation for Hierarchical Input-Process-Output Chart. A type of flow chart that uses standardised flowchart symbols to show the data flow through an organisation or program.

Hoff, Ted: An exceptional engineer who, as leader of a re., search team at Intel, conceptualised and developed the Intel 4004 microprocessor, the first of its kind. In the early 1970s, Intel were trying to design a processor and circuit board that needed to accommodate at least 2000 transistors. Hoffs approach was to rely more on software than hardware, enabling the Intel design to incorporate the entire processor on a single integrated circuit, introducing the word "microprocessor" to the language.

Hollerith Code: This code, developed by Herman Hollerith, is used to enter data on a punched card. Hollerith designed the code specifically for use in tabulating the data from the 1890 census in America. The code was revised in 1994 into its present 80 column format. In 1896 Hollerith formed the Tabulating Company, a successful enterprise that was later sold and, after a few mergers, became International Business Machines (IBM).

Holy war: An neverending argument between intractable sides, such as over gun control, abortion, or IBM vs. Mac. There are usually special talk newsgroups set up for the people who can't resist arguing with their opposites, and it's considered bad form to bring up a holy war topic in an inappropriate forum.

$HOME: In UNIX, a variable that serves as an abbreviation home directory.

Home directory: The directory allotted to your specific account, where you start off when you log into your UNIX account, and where you store your files.

Home page: On the Web, a starting page with links to other related pages. Many people have personal home pages with biographical information and a hotlist of favorite Web destinations.

Homogeneous network: A network that includes only one part of computer, operating system, network card, and so on, and there fore a single network protocol.

Hop: Each short, individual trip that packets make many times over, from router to router, on their way to their destinations.

Hop count: The number of hops it will take for a packet to make it from a source to a destination.

Horizontal Motion Index (HMI): The minimum distance that a print head can be advanced in a horizontal direction. This is a measure of the resolution of the printer.

Host: A computer on a network that allows many users access at once. If you connect to the Internet by dialing up a provider via a modem, then the computer you log into is your local host.

Host Computer: A computer, usually a mainframe, which controls (that is, supervises) other computers in a network or complex computer system.

Host name: Also *hostname,* the leftmost portion of a fully qualified domain name, uniquely identifying a specific computer on a network in a subdomain in a domain.

Hotlist: A list of frequent destinations, or sites, arranged on a menu, such as a list of Web pages.

HTML: *Hypertext markup language,* the hypertext language used in Web pages. It consists of regular text and tags that tell the browser what to do when a link is activated.

HTTP: *Hypertext transport protocol,* the Internet protocol that defines how a Web server respond to requests for files, made via anchors and URLs.

Hub: In networks arranged with star topology, the central connecting device, a device, that allows a network to add workstations by extending the transmission signal.

HWD: An acronym for the physical dimensions of hardware (HWD = height/width/depth). For example an external 3.5" floppy disk drive may be referred to as 6/17/31 HWD (6cm high, 17cm wide, 31cm deep). The units, in this case centimetres, are generally not stated. Assume inches for USA manufacturers, centimetres elsewhere.

Hypermedia: An extension of the concept of hypertext to include pictures, sounds, movies, and so on, along with text and links to other documents.

Hypermedia link: A link from one document to another, from an anchor to a named location, or from an anchor to another form of media entirely, such as a picture, sound, or movie.

Hypertext link: A link from one text document to another or from a text anchor to a named location.

Hyphenation: The process of hyphenating text so that it will more easily fit into the prescribed text block size. Many word processors and desktop publishing packages offer automatic hyphenation. These use specialised dictionaries to determine whether a word should be hyphenated or not.

I

IBM: International Business Machines, a large, US based, multinational corporation. IBM has been the instigator of many de-facto industry standards and is generally seen as an industry leader.

Icon: An on-screen symbol that is used, to represent a menu choice or a task being processed.

IEEE: Abbreviation for Institute of Electrical and Electronics Engineers.

IF: A programming statement used in many high level languages which is used to make a comparison between different parameters of the program.

Ignore: On IRC or in any other type of chat, to screen out the contributions of a participant who is annoying you.

IMAP: *Internet Message Access Protocol,* a protocol for the storage and retrieval of e-mail, not yet a widespread standard.

Imminent Death of the Net Predicted: A parody of the perennial warnings that traffic on the Net has gotten to be too much.

Inbox: Also *in box* and *in-box* a file in which a mail program stores incoming e-mail messages.

Include: To copy some or all of the message to which you are responding. Most e-mail programs and newsreaders will add a character such as > before each line of included text.

#include <disclaimer.h>: A C joke that appears in sig blocks, meaning that a standard disclaimer should be understood to have been included there.

Include war: A flame war in which so many previous posts have been included that it's impossible to follow the argument amidst all the >s

Incremental Backup: A backup process that only updates those flies that have changed since the last backup operation. This is a useful, time saving feature.

Indent: In word processing this refers to reducing the size of a text block, or parts of a text block, to set that section apart from the rest of the text.

Index: A file in a directory at a site that describes the contents of the directory; An archie database; A default Web page that a Web server provides when no file is specified.

Industrial Espionage: The stealing/copying of unpublished or proprietary information from an organisation or individual, with the objective of gaining benefit from that information. New processes, product designs and marketing plans are common targets. Industrial espionage is increasingly hard to thwart given the small size and portability of many secondary storage devices. Such devices allow an employee to remove a vast amount of data from an organisation's premises undetected.

INET: An annual conference put on by the Internet Society; An abbreviation for Internet.

Infinite loop: A computer process that repeats forever due to a programming error, causing the computer to hang. The instructions on the back of many a shampoo bottle—lather, rinse, repeat—would cause an infinite loop in a computer.

Info: A common username for a mailbot providing information about a network, service provider, or informa-tion service.

Info-Mac archives: A huge collection of Macintosh software at the sumex-aim. stanford.edu FTP site, in the /info-mac directory. It's also mirrored at wuarchive. wustl.edu in the /mirrors/info-mac directory.

Information: This is a generic term applied to any knowledge of a particular fact, event or situation.

Information agent: A program that searches databases for information without requiring that the user know where the information is stored.

Information Management: The gathering, storage, or.ganisation and use of information. Information is the basis of most organisational activities and plays a vital part in managing an organisation.

Information Overload: This occurs when a person receives more, information than he or she can effectively absorb or deal with.

Information pooper-highway: Some people think that the Internet won't reach its ultimate potential until computers are taken into the bathroom as easily as newspapers.

Information Science: The study of the collection, manage-ment and organisation of information and information systems.

Information wants to be free: A slogan popular on the Internet, suggesting that it is impossible,, ultimately, to hoard information, as it finds its way into general availability much as water proverbially seeks its own level.

Info-server: An e-mail address that triggers a mail server, responding to messages that contain key words by sending stored information.

In-house: Activities that are completed by an organisation using its own resources. Some examples of usage of the phrase are, "we can use inhouse expertise for that programming" or "we can do that disk conversion in-house".

Initgame: An IRC variation on the guessing game called Botticelli, in which one participant changes their nick to the initials of a famous or fictional person and the other participants ask yes-or-no questions trying to guess the secret, identity. Winner gets to start the next game.

Initialization string: A string of seemingly nonsense, characters sent to a modem to get it ready to make a connection.

Ink Jet Printer: A non-impact printer that shoots minute bubbles of ink on to the print surface to form the image. This is a very quiet printer that lends itself to colour output since it is easy to have more than one source of ink.

Input: The process of entering data into a computer. Traditionally this has been a manual process, performed by computer operators, but much of this work is now automated. For example, stock control in many large shops is now achieved by direct data entry from cash register transactions. Similarly, bank account records are updated by transactions conducted by members of the public through automatic teller machines (ATMs).

Input Device: Any hardware, such as a keyboard, scanner, digitiser, barcode reader, light-pen, mouse, ATM, remote sensing equipment etc, that generates computer compatible input.

Inquiry Screen: A screen design philosophy used where the user may not necessarily be computer literate and/or where rapid information retrieval is required. Inquiry Screens are commonly used in large libraries for accessing books by title/subject/author etc. They use a simple command structure and a user-friendly interface.

Insert mode: In text editors such as vi, a special mode the user has to switch into insert text.

Installation: The process of setting up hardware and/or software for use by a particular organisation or on a particular computer system. Software is increasingly setup by running a special install program.

Institute of Electrical and Electronic Engineering (IEEE): A professional organization among other things, has defined a number of networking standards, such as the 802.x protocols.

Instruction: A command that is recognised by the CPU (processor). Commands are usually generated by a single step in a computer program, often several instructions may be generated per line of code. Each processor has its own instruction set and these may not necessarily be compatible with other processors.

Instruction Word: A combination of an opcode (an instruction) and an operand, which specifies the data (memory locations) that will take part in the process called for. In machine language this combination produces a typical instruction word such as that shown below:

0100 0101101001110010

Here the first four digits are the opcode and the remainder is the operand. If only four digits are used for the opcode then only 16 different opcodes are possible.

For convenience the instruction word is stored in hex format (the above instruction word would then become 4 5A72). The complete instruction word may, for example, tell the microprocesor to fetch the word stored in address 5A72, add it to the number already stored in the accumulator and store the result in the accumulator.

Integer: A number that does not have any decimal points, also known as a whole number. Integers are typically used to represent a telephone number, a postcode, the number of people in an organisation etc. The following numbers are integers 47, 3188, 2001. Program variables can be declared in the program header as being integers.

Integrated Circuit: An electronic assembly that contains many hundreds, if not thousands/hundreds of thousands, of individual electronic components (transistors, diodes, etc). Integrated circuit technology has had a major impact on the evolution of computers, enabling them to become both smaller and faster. An integrated circuit (abbreviation IC) is manufactured using photochemical techniques on a silicon substrate, a highly automated process that has ensured that the price of most electronic devices has fallen dramatically over the past twenty years. Silicon is used because of its favourable chemistry (a Group 4 element on the boundary between metals and nonmetals, silicon is a semiconductor).

Integrated Services Digital Net Work: A service provided by a common carrier which combines voice, data and video communications. Abbreviation ISDN.

Intel: An American developer/manufacturer of highly successful IC designs. One of the pioneers of today's microprocessors.

Intelligent agent: A type of computer program that can handle a user's mail, database searches, file transfers, and so on over the Internet with out the user having to oversee the process directly or even remain connected to the Net.

Interactive: Said of programs or environments, able to respond and give feedback to a user and to take instruction from user commands.

Interactive Menu: A menu philosophy that poses questions on a one-at-a-time basis. As each question is answered the next one is placed on the screen. Often used in Business Information Processing.

Interactive Processing: The processing of data as and when it becomes available, not in a batch at the end of a data entry session.

Interagency Interim National Research and Education Network (IINREN): A set of network and operating, system protocols under development for the National Research and Education Network.

Interblock Gap: The space between a group (block) of records on a computer tape. **Interface:** An item of hardware interposed between two other devices.

Interior Gateway Protocol (IGP): A protocol that defines how routing information is distributed among routers in a network.

Interleave: This is one of the protocols used when data is written to disk. It may seem logical to write data on contiguous sectors but in many cases this is not the best method. Because of microprocessor and/or read/write delays it may be beneficial to write the data on sector 1, and then wait for sector 4. The gap between sectors is taken up by processing time and/or data read times during which time sector 2 has been and gone from under the read/write head. Just coming over the horizon is sector 4 and it will be quicker (more efficient) to write to this sector than wait the latency period for sector 2 to come round again.

In practice many computers aim for a 1:1 Interleave, indicating that contiguous sectors are in fact used. However the fact that a 1.1 Interleave is used may not necessarily indicate efficiency. The Interleave capability of a computer is setup during low-level formatting.

intermittent: Said of a connection, riot constant, occurring irregularly.

Internal Command: In MS-DOS this is a command that is available via the generic command processor and does not require the loading of any executable file.

Internal modem: A modem chip mounted on a board installed inside a computer.

International Organization for Standardization (ISO): An international standards organization attempting to foster international cooperation in science, engineering, and technology. Creator of the OSI Model.

Internet addressing: In IP, transmission of data and headers is done as shown in Figure. Octet I is transmitted first, then octet 2, and so on. An IP address has two parts: network number and host number. The IP layer recognizes the IP address only. IP address classes are Class A, Class B, Class C, Class D, and Class E. The main distinction among Class A, Class B, and Class C is in the division between network number and host number, also referred to as the *rest field*.

Internet Architecture Board (IAB): A group that oversees the maintenance of TCP/IP protocols and promulgates other Internet standards.

Internet Assigned Numbers Authority (IANA): A group that assigns the standard numbers used for ports, sockets, and so on. Assigned numbers can be found in the Internet document called STD2.

Internet-Draft (I-D): Draft documents written by the Internet Engineering Task Force dealing with potential problems and networking developments. They are archived at the ftp.internic.net anonymous FTP site.

Internet Engineering Steering Group (IESG): A group that manages the Internet Engineering Task Force and reviews Internet standards.

Internet Engineering Task Force (IETF): A voluntary group made up of researchers that studies technical problems and proposes solutions to the Internet Architecture Board.

Internet Experiment Note (IEN): A now-obsolete series of reports on the development of the Internet, parallel to the RFCs.

Internet Hunt: A monthly contest consisting of ten questions whose answers must be dug up on the Internet. The contest is reachable by gopher via gopher. cic.net in the hunt directory.

Internet Monthly Report (IMR): A monthly publication about the Internet, produced for the Internet Research Task Force.

Internet Protocol (IP): The protocol that handles routing of datagrams from one Internet host to another. It works along with the Transmission Control Protocol to ensure that data is trasmitted accurately across the Internet. The IP is a connectionless best-effort packet delivery service. In this protocol, there is no end-to-end guaranteed delivery, acknowledgment, flow control, retransmission, or error recovery. This protocol tries its best to deliver packets to the destination. The frames are discarded as a last resort. If connectionoriented support is required, then it must be provided by the upper layers. The IP layer deals with fouroctet IP addresses.

The IP datagram is as shown in Figure, consisting of the IP header and the data portion. The first field in the IP header is the *version* of IP, which version is provided to furnish details of the IP software. Like any technology, changes do occur to account for advances. The present version is 4. The version field alerts the system to these changes and facilitates compatibility. The IP header length is in multiples of 32 bits. The *length* ·field extends from the version field to the beginning of the data portion. Total length is inclusive of the IP header and data, and is measured in octets. Because the length field is 16 bits, it can accommodate up to 65,535 octets. However, there is also a restriction that hosts must be able to accept IP datagrams larger than 576 octets.

Though IP imposes an upper limit of 65,535, protocols used in the lower levels impose their own restrictions. For example, Ethernet has its. minimum of 64 octets and maximum of 1518 octet frame length limitations. So the length of datagrams sent in networks will be guided by limitations other than the ones imposed by the IP layer. The *type of service* (TOS) field is one octet long. The first three bits indicate *precedence,* for which different levels are defined. High-precedence traffic is regarded as more important than low-precedence traffic.

Bits 6 and 7 of the TOS field are reserved for future use, and they are set to zero. However, RFC 1349 redefines the TOS field. Here the TOS field is taken as four bits; the last bit is labeled Must Be Zero (MBZ), and this bit is unused. TOS values mentioned in Table are the values which will be tried. If the network cannot provide the TOS requested, then values used will be those of the network.

When a datagram is larger than the size that can be handled by a network, then a gateway converts the datagram into smaller-size fragments which are multiples of eight. As an example, the IP datagram shown in Figure can be converted to smaller datagrams as shown. This action of forming smaller datagrams out of a large one is known as *fragmentation,* also sometimes known as segmentation. However, these fragments are reassembled only in the destination host and not in the intermediate gateways.

The *identification* field is 16 bits in length. It has three bits of the *flag* field and 13 bits of *fragment offset*. In the flag field, the fist bit (bit 0) is set to 0. Bit I has two options. If it is set to 0, then it indicates that the datagram may be fragmented. If it is set to 1, then the datagram cannot be fragmented. Bit 2 of flag again has two options. When fragmentation is done, this bit in the last fragment is set to 0. However, in other fragments, this bit is 1, indicating that there are more fragments of the datagram. The other IP field, *fragment offset,* furnishes the offset of the datagram, which is in units of eight octets. The first fragment has a fragment offset of 0. The next IP header field, known as the *time to live* (TTL) field, is eight bits long and has time in seconds. TTL specifies how long a datagram remains in a system. Because a gateway is able to process a packet in less than a second, the TTL count is reduced by one. In such a case, the TTL counter becomes a maximum allowable count of hops for a packet to reach the destination host. When the TTL becomes zero, then a datagram destroys itself. This process is also known as *self-destruction* and prevents a datagram from making unnecessary cycles in the network.

The *protocol* field has the protocol number of the upper layer. For example, ICMP has a protocol number of 1, and the protocol number for TCP is 6. Assigned numbers of higher-layer protocols are furnished in Reference. The *header checksum* field provides the checksum of the IP header field only, and does not include the checksum of the data portion. It is obtained by adding the ones complement of different fields and then taking the ones complement of the sum. The source and destination IP addresses are the addresses of the sender and receiver. The destination IP address does not refer to the addresses of intermediate gateways.

The *options* field must be implemented in all hosts and gateways, but it is optional in datagrams. There are two types of options field, Case 1 and Case 2. In Case 1, the *option type* field is one octet long. Case 2 has a one-octet option type, one octet of *option length,* and the option data. The option length octet includes the length of the option data and two octets that include one octet of option type and one octet of option length fields. The option field has one bit of flag, two bits of option class, and five bits of option number.

One bit of flag indicates whether the option field is copied into fragments on fragmentation. If it is zero, then the option field is not copied and if it is set to one, then the option field is copied into all the fragments. The option field is quite useful for adding a variety of features, but options cannot be used unless they are accepted by the general Internet community. The *padding* field is used to ensure that the IP header aligns on a 32-bit boundary.

Internet control message protocol(ICMP) ICMP is used for communicating error or control messages from one host to another host or from routers (gateways) to the host. ICMP is required in every IP layer. The ICMP message occupies the data portion of the IP. It has a header of its own and data. For an ICMP message, the protocol field in the IP header is set to 1. For ICMP, TOS is always set to 0000. The source address refers to the host address or router address which generated the ICMP message. The destination address is the address of the host or router to which the ICMP message must be sent.

The ICMP field always has an ICMP type field, which distinguishes different ICMP messages. There is also a code field, which gives more details about messages, and the checksum field, which furnishes the checksum for the ICMP message portion only.

The IP header and first 64 bits of the original datagram refer to the header and the data of the layer above ICMP. The layer above can be either TCP or UDP. The first 64 bits of data are used for matching processes which may use the ICMP message. The ICMP message is quite useful for discovering hosts and routers. The Packet InterNet Groper (PING) is used for checking the connectivity of a host with a remote host and getting the details of a host. It is also quite useful for network management. PING is an echo request and echo reply, and is useful for gathering data on hosts and routers. The ICMP message for an echo request and echo reply is shown in Figure. When an echo request is to be sent, the ICMP type is 8. The destination address is the address of the router or host IP which must send an echo of the message back to the sender.

Identifier and sequence numbers are used for identifying and matching a message and its replies. If code is 0, then both identifier and sequence number may be 0. As we have seen earlier, echo request and echo reply can be used to gather data and statistics on the network and hosts and routers.

Transmission control protocol (TCP): TCP is a connection-oriented, reliable, packet-switching protocol used for communication between processes in host computers. These host computers are distinct and are part of a communication network. The data transfer is full-duplex, which means that the sender sends data in one direction and can simultaneously receive data from the opposite direction. One of the strengths of the TCP protocol is its flexibility. It does not specifically mandate any protocol for the layer above it or the layer below. Usually, in Internet, the lower-layer protocol is IP. TCP is a stream-oriented protocol, and the combination of TCP layer data and headers is known as a *segment*.

An important concept in TCP is that of a connection. TCP provides for a set of addresses or *ports* within each host. Many processes can be associated with a port. The IP address and port number identify a *socket*. A pair of sockets identify a *connection*. Before communication can take place, a connection must be established between processes. This connection is referred to as a *virtual circuit*, which is analogous to a telephone connection being formed before the start of a conversation.

In a network, segments of data may be damaged or corrupted, lost, duplicated, or delivered out of order. To account for this, there is provision for acknowledgment and retransmission. When data is sent by a sender, the sequence number of the first octet of data in the segment is also sent. At the same time, the sender starts a timer. The receiving end sends an acknowledgment number. This acknowledgment refers to the sequence number of the next expected data octet to be sent by the sender. However, if the acknowledgment is not received before the timer runs out, then the sender retransmits the segment.

There is also provision for a checksum of the data to identify whether the data has been corrupted. We have seen earlier that IP does not provide a checksum of the data; it provides for a checksum of the IP header only. So TCP takes account of this fact to provide a reliable communication mechanism.

Flow control is achieved by means of a variable window that can be sent along with an acknowledgment by a receiver. If the receiver does not have much buffer space left, then it sends a smaller window. Conversely, where the receiver is willing to accept and process data at a faster rate, it adjusts the window to a larger number than the existing one. The destination IP address identifies the destination host, and the source IP address identifies the source host address. In this figure, SA1 is the source host IP address, and DA1 is the destination host IP address. The applications Al, A2, and A3 are the source ports. It is assumed that they want to communicate with destination ports B1, B2, and B3, respectively. The process in Host 1, where applications are combined, is analogous to multiplexing, and the process in Host 2, where they are directed to the respective ports, is similar to demultiplexing seen in the data transmissions across a transmission medium.

A TCP segment has a TCP header part and a data part. The TCP header has the following fields:

Source port number: A 16-bit field, containing a source port number.

Destination port number: Also a 16-bit field, with a destination port number where a data segment must be sent.

Sequence number: The sequence number of a data octet of a segment that is being sent from a sender. In the case of synchronization or when the SYN bit is set, it is the *initial sequence number* (ISN). The first octet of data starts from ISN + 1. Here note that the ISN need not always start with 0, or the first octet sequence number need not always start with 1. The sequence number is a 32-bit field.

Acknowledgment number: A 32-bit field, always sent once a connection has been established. This is the number of the first data octet which a receiver expects to receive next. For example, if a receiver has received data up to 100 octets, the receiver puts the acknowledgment number as 101. The receiver next expects a segment in which the data octet starts with 101.

Data offset: A four-bit field. A TCP header is a multiple of 32 bits. This field contains the length of the TCP header measured in terms of 32 bits. In a segment, data offset indicates where the data starts.

Reserved: Intended for future use and set to 0. It is six bits in length. It is a good idea to provide for a reserved field in any protocol. When technology changes or new tech-nologies are incorporated, these reserved bits can beused. The first six fields in the following list are all one-bit fields.

URG: Urgent pointer significant field. TCP has provided for sending out-of-band urgent data. When this bit is set, the receiver is expected to process this segment first, interrupting all other activities. When the URG bit is set, the urgent pointer fieid has relevance.

ACK. Acknowledgment significant field. When this field is set, an acknowledgment number is sent.

PSH: Push function field. When this field is set, the sender is expected to send whatever data is available in the buffer instead of waiting for the send buffer to be filled up.

RST. Used for resetting a connection. When this bit is set, depending on the states of sender and receiver, actions are taken. For example, reset is sent when a segment for another connection is received.

SYN: For synchronizing sequence numbers. This is used in the beginning to establish a connection by means of a three-way handshake.

FIN: Used for closing a connection.

Window: A 16-bit field. Because the data in IP segments are in terms of octets, window states the number of octets which a receiver is willing to receive, starting from one.

Checksum: A 16-bit field. The checksum is calculated and includes a TCP pseudo header and TCP segment. The TCP pseudo header has source and destination addresses, eight bits set to 0, the protocol, and TCP length. The pseudo header is used for computing the checksum and is not transmitted while transmitting data. That is the reason for naming it a pseudo header. Here, TCP length is the sum of the TCP header and TCP data. This TCP length does not, however, include 12 octets of the TCP pseudo header. For checksum, header and text octets must be even. To make these even, sometimes the last octet is padded with 0. To form the checksum, the ones complement of the TCP header is taken, then the ones complement of the result is taken.

Urgent pointer: Provides positive offset from the sequence number in a segment. This points to data offset following urgent data. As mentioned earlier, this field is taken into consideration only if the URG bit is set. This is a 16-bit field.

Options: A variable-length field, with length in multiples of eight bits. Here, too, there are two options: *Case 1*: Has one octet of option; *Case 2*: Has one octet of option, one octet of option length, and variable-length options data. Here, as in the IP, length includes two octets due to the option and option length.

User datagram protocol (UDP) SNMP, Internet Name Server, and Trivial File Transfer use the UDP protocol. This is a connectionless datagram service. UDP, in turn, depends upon the connectionless IP layer. As a result, there is no guarantee that data will be delivered; there may be duplicate frames sent, or data may be received in an order different from the order in which they were sent. Also, there is no acknowledgment that data has been delivered. However, if an application wishes to provide services that are available in a connection oriented service, it is the responsibility of the application to incorporate them in upper-layer software. In UDP, an application that wants to transmit data to another application uses a scheme similar to TCP The data of the application are initially enveloped with a UDP header. Then, at the IP layer, the IP header is appended. In the NI layer, the network header is appended to the IP frame. This frame is transmitted over the Internet to the other end. On the receiving end, the NI layer removes the network layer header, and the IP layer strips off the IP header. The UDP layer, in turn, removes the UDP header and routes data to the appropriate application. If there is a mismatch or the proper frame is not received, the ICMP message can be sent to the original application with causes for the error.

The UDP datagram is as shown in Figure. It has 16 bits each of source port and destination numbers. The length field contains the number of octets of the UDP frame and includes the length of the UDP frame headers. The next field in the UDP header is the checksum field, which is an optional field. If it is not used, then this field has zeros; however, if the checksum field is used, it contains the ones complement of the checksum derived from a pseudo header.

The UDP pseudo header is similar to the TCP pseudo header. The UDP pseudo header has four octets each of source IP address and destination IP address, zero padding, protocol, and UDP length. One octet of zero padding is done to make the UDP frame a multiple of two. One octet protocol field is 17 for IP, and the two-byte UDP length field is the length of the UDP datagram in octets. However ' the UDP length field does not include the length of the pseudo header. Thus, an application that wants to send data needs to know the IP addresses of source and destination beforehand in the UDP layer itself.

The use of checksum is mostly guided by the application. Note here that IP uses only the header checksum; it does not use the checksum over the IP data portion. Hence, if some validation of whether the UDP frame is the correct one is required, then the checksum in UDP is required. In some cases, we may not want to have the overhead of computing the checksum., since the loss of some UDP frames may not matter much. One such case is that of monitoring the performance of a resource, where the loss of a UDP datagram may not mean much. Also, in some cases, a network may be very reliable, without the risk of losing frames. In other cases, the application may be critical and the loss of a frame may lead to problems. In such cases, it is better to use checksum. Also, when a network is unreliable, it is appropriate to use the cheeksum to make sure that the data delivered is correct.

Address resolution protocol (ARP) We have seen that Internet knows only the IP address. Let us investigate how an IP packet is sent to the other end. An IP packet has a destination IP address. Then the local host looks at the ARP table and checks where the destination is. An ARP table is a sort of lookup table which has a mapping between an IP address and its corresponding physical address. Then the NI layer inserts the actual physical address of the destination host. The Ethernet or tokenring frame has this destination physical address. On the destination side, this Ethernet frame is stripped of its physical address and routed to the right IP layer. When this happens, the destination is in the same network. However, it is possible that the destination could be another network, in which case, instead of the physical address of the destination host, the physical address of the IP router is appended in the Ethernet frame. In the IP router, a check is again made with a routing table to see where the destination IP address is. If there are many hops or steps required before a destination can be reached, then the physical addresses of the IP routers are successively inserted. In the last IP router, the destination host physical address is retrieved from the destination IP address to route the IP packet to the correct destination.

The next issue is how to build an ARP table. This is done by broadcasting an ARP request packet, which has a source IP address, source physical address, and destination IP address. When this packet is broadcast, each host examines the IP address and looks whether it matches its own IP address. If it matches, the host puts its IP address and physical address in the source. The earlier source IP and physical addresses are transferred to the destination IP address and the destination physical address, and the response is sent back.

In the original host that sent the ARP request packet, the ARP table now has the mapping of the destination IP address and physical address. It is possible that no host has a matching IP address when an ARP request packet is sent. In such a case, the IP address is not, known.

The manner in which the IP packet handles cases in which mapping between the IP address and physical address is not known is, implementation dependent. In some cases, when the mapping is not there, the IP packet is queued and an ARP request packet is sent. When the destination physical address becomes known, the ARP request packet is received. The IP packet is dequeued and sent to the destination. If the address is not known, the IP layer discards the packets. In some cases, these IP packets may not be queued. If the IP packets are not delivered, the upper layers are alerted by *timeouts.*

Reverse address resolution protocol (RARP) RARP is the reverse process of ARP, in which mapping is from a physical address to the IP address. A station may have its physical address; it sends a RARP to a server giving its IP address, and the server maps the IP address and sends back the physical address.

Internet Research Steering Group (IRSG): A group that manages the Internet Research Task Force.

Internet Research Task Force (IRTF): A voluntary group that projects longterm issues and problems for the Internet and proposes solutions and new directions, reporting to the Internet Architecture Board.

Internet Service List: An exhaustive list of Internet services, maintained by Scott Yanoff and available via anonymous FTP.

Internet Society (ISOC): A nonprofit organization that promotes the use of the Internet in academic and research communities and supports networking research, publishing the *Internet Society News* and putting on the INET conference every year.

Internet Talk Radio (ITR): A set of audio programs, similar to radio broadcasts, distributed over the Internet via the MBONE.

Internet tools: A set of utility programs that can use various Internet facilities and that have interoperability.

Internet Underground Music Archive (IUMA): A database of bands, including sound clips, video clips, information, and many other musicrelated links.

Internetwork Packet Exchange (IPX): Novell's Netware network layer protocol that specifies addressing, routing, and switching packets between a server and workstations and across interconnected LANs. Encapsulated TX packets can be carried by Ethernet packets and token ring frames.

InterNIC: Short for the Internet Net work Information Center, a service of the National Science Foundation. It provides information about the Internet and registers domain names.

interoperability: The ability of devices by different manufacturers or as part of different computer systems to communication and share information over a network.

Interpreter: Software that reads each line of program code and converts it on a line by line basis into machine code.

Interrupt: An instruction to the CPU. This instruction suspends the current task in favour of a new task. The previous task is resumed when the CPU becomes free again.

InterSLIP: Macintosh SLIP software, developed by InterCon Systems Corporation.

Intuitive Command: A command whose name is indicative of the outcome of the command.

IP address: Internet Protocol address that uniquely identifies each computer on the Internet, made up of four numbers separated by three dots.

J

Jargon file: A list of hacker jargon and slang—compiled and maintained collectively since the 1960s—with excellent definitions, great humour, and lots of interesting anecdotes.

Job control language: A batch oriented control language used on mainframe and minicomputers. It identifies data files to be used for processing, storage locations to be used and the sequence of each job

Joe: A UNIX text editor.

Joint Photographics Experts Group: An ISO committee that proposed the JPEG image compression standard.

JPEG: A compressed file format for images that is more efficient than CIF (but newer and therefore not so widespread).

Jumper: A temporary wire linking two or more hardware connections. Jumpers are usually flexible wires, often with simple connectors at each end, and are often used for faultfinding or for introducing optional facilities, for example, different lock speeds, to computers. The word jumper, like many others in computer jargon, is borrowed from the communications industry.

Jupiter: (v) To kill an IRC 'bot or kick a user and then keep the 'bot or user from reconnecting by adopting its nick.

Justification: A process used in desktop publishing, typesetting and word processing which ensures that the text block is even on each side, that is, the left and right margins are a straight line. Justification is achieved by manipulating character widths, the space between characters, the space between words and by kerning.

K

K: In computer science, an abbreviation for a value equal to 210, or 1, 024.

kbps: An abbreviation for kilobits pc second, a measure-ment of transmission speed.

Kermit: A transmission protocol for transferring files bet-ween computers.

Kernel: A part of a memory resident program. A kernel is the core of such a program and remains in memory (RAM) whilst other parts of the program may be removed from memory and only recalled from disk in response to specific commands.

Kerning: A technique used in desktop publishing, type-setting and word processing which attempts to improve the appearance of text.

Key: 1. In encryption, a phrase or string that allows you to decrypt encrypted text. In publickey encryption, there are two kinds of keys, public keys and private keys; 2. A key word.

Keyboard: A typewriter-like console used for comm-unicating with the computer and for entering text and data. The keyboard in most common use is the QWERTY Board. There are many proprietary variations of the QWERTY Board but the basic layout of the alphanumerics remains the same. The QWERTY board is not the most efficient in ergonomic terms but remains the most commonly used keyboard design. The QWERTY layout originates from the earliest typewriters where the main concern was the mechanics of the machine and the minimisation of typewriter printhead clashes.

Keyboard Initialisation: A procedure that is run during the booting of many computers. Keyboard Initialisation is started by ROM BIOS (Read Only Memory, Basic Input Output System) to check that the keyboard is plugged in and that the correct scan codes are used. Successful keyboard initialisation is usually signalled by the Num Lock LED coming on.

Keyboard Skills: The ability to use a computer keyboard effectively and efficiently. Keyboard skills are considered essential for computer professionals and increasingly a life skill for everyone as they are often required in daily life.

Keyboard Template: A plastic proforma that fits over the keys of a computer keyboard, providing quick and easy reference to particular software application key functions. Keyboard templates are increasingly supplied as part of a Software package.

Key encryption: A form of encryption that relies upon keys for the encrypting, and decrypting of messages or files.

Key Punch Operator: A person who operates a key punch machine. This was one of the early methods of entering data into a computer. The key punch machine converted the typed entries into code on a series of paper cards, which were then read by an electromechanical card reader.

Keyword: 1. In a database search, a word to search for in target documents—hits must include the key word; 2. In online services, a word used to jump directly to a topic area.

Kgbvax: One of the machines on the bang path of the famous April Fool's kremvax post.

Kibo: The username of James F. Parry, acclaimed by some as the first deity of the Internet. Kibo reportedly notes every mention of his name on Usenet and follows up worthy posts. He is also the founder of HappyNet. Students of kibology can read more on the subject in the alt.religion.kibology newsgroup.

kibology: The religion of Kibo. Its main doctrine is You're Allowed. Only Spot, Kibo's dog, is Not Allowed.

Kibo number: Also *Kibo #,* a number that represents how close you are to Kibo in terms of e-mail. Kibo's Kibo number is 0. Anyone who has gotten mail from Kibo has the Kibo number 1. Mail from someone with a lower Kibo number than yours lowers your Kibo number to that person's Kibo number plus 1.

Kiboze: (v) To grep the newsfeed to find every single post that mentions the key word you're grepping for.

Kick: (v) To eject a participant from an IRC conversation and prevent the user from rejoining.

Kill file: A file containing search instructions for auto-matically killing or autoselecting Usenet posts. Sometimes called a bozo filter, a kill file can be used to screen out annoying posters and avoid uninteresting threads.

Kilobit: One thousand (2^ 10) bits. This term is often used to describe the memory capacity of RAM chips, for example, "this is a 256 kilobit chip".

Kilobits per second: A measurement of the speed of a medium, meaning the number of kilobits that can pass through the medium in one second.

Kilobyte: A unit which equals 1024 (2^ 10) bytes. A byte is eights bits of information and is roughly synonymous with one character of data storage. On most computers a byte is the smallest amount of memory that can be reached via the address bus.

Kluge: *(klooj,* n) The original and more phonetically correct spelling of *kludge,* a clumsily assembled program or feature of a program that functions well enough but is not elegant, similar to the noncomputer expression *jury-rigged.*

Knowbot Information Services (KIS): An experimental information service on the Net, intended to function as a robotic librarian that can search databases and, among other things, help find e-mail addresses.

L

LAN: (n) *Local area network,* a computer network, usually confined to a single office that allows for the sharing of files and other resources among several users and makes interoperability among various systems possible.

LAN adapter: A card installed into a PC to attach it to a LAN.

Land Information System: A computer system (hardware and software) which is used to analyse land management information, for example, the distribution of natural resources, land usage patterns, property ownership, rateable values etc.

LAN Workplace: Novell's TCP/IP client software for Macintosh and DOS com puters.

Landing Zone: An area on a hard disk platter reserved for 64 parking” the read/write head. Early designs of hard disk required a manual “parking” command but this is now included as the last action in the dying moments of power availa bility. The landing zone is a non data storage area, and is often the highest numbered track/cylinder on the disk.

Landmark: A proprietary hardware/software evaluation system developed in America.

Landscape: This refers to the hard copy images. Landscape indicates that the job was printed across the long side of the page rather than the vertical orientation which is far more common.

LapTop Computer: A PC specifically designed to be easily portable (light and compact) and to be easily usable on a person's lap. LapTop computers started out as very basic machines but many now have very powerful’ processing capabilities.

Laser Printer: A high resolution printer, typically 300 dpi, which uses electrostatic techniques and laser beams to produce images. The printer uses laser beams to create an electrostatic charge on selected parts of the image surface which is then transferred to the print surface. Dry powder ink, usually referred to as "toner", is attracted to the charged area and forms the appropriate image.

Latency: The amount of time required, on average, for the required data to appear under the read\write head of a disk drive. If the required data has just passed under the read\write head at the time of data request then the latency period will be close to the maximum possible. A full revolution of the disk platter is necessary before the data again appears under the read\write head. On a hard disk spinning at 3600 revolutions per minute this will be approximately 16 milliseconds.

Led: The UNIX ftp command to change the local directory (as opposed to the working directory at the ftp host site).

Leading: The spacing between lines of text measured in points. The leading or a given point size would always be greater than the point size of the font. Leading and font point sizes are often quoted together to give an impression, to the trained mind, of how the finished product would look on paper. The text in this book is set in 11/12 Times Roman, indicating an 11 point typeface with 12 points of leading.

Leaf: 1. In network architecture, a computer that receives a signal from a more central computer but does not pass a signal along to a more remote computer, 2. *In (audio* cassette) tape trees, a participant who receives a copy of the tape being distributed but does not make copies of the tape for anyone else.

Leaf site: A Usenet computer that receives a newsfeed from another site but does not distribute news to any other computers.

League for Programming Freedom: A group that opposes software patents and copyrights; information available via anonymous FTP at prep.ai.mit. edu in the pub/lpf directory or by email at league@prep.ai.mit. edu.

Learning Curve: A graph showing the relationship between continued practice at a given task and the resulting gains in proficiency, speed and accuracy. Sometimes called an experience curve. Software users may talk of "an easy learning curve" or "a long learning curve".

Leased line: A telephone line leased from the telephone company to provide a permanent connection from a LAN to an Internet service provider or to a WAN.

Letterbomb: An e-mail message containing either escape characters that can lock up certain types or terminals, or harmful commands to be interpreted by the user's shell.

Lexis/Nexis: A proprietary system of searchable databases of legal briefs (Lexis) and newspaper and magazine articles (Nexis)

Lharc: A file compression program for DOS.

.lhz: A file extension that indicates lharc compression.

Library: A collection of pre-written, pretested program modules that can be called upon to form part of a new program. Libraries are usually stored on disk and are made available during compiletime and runtime as required.

Library catalogues: Most university and library catalogs are available via telnet. Hytelnet index of library catalogs.

Library of Congress: The main repository of information of the U. S. government, available by telnet at locis. loc.gov.

Light Emitting Diode: An electronic device that emits light when a voltage is applied to it. They are often used as a "Power On" indicator on computers and computer hardware.

Light Pen: A hand held device, connected to a computer, that can read barcodes. They are commonly used in supermarkets and other retail stores. Light pens can also be used as a pointing device in conjunction with a computer monitor. The pen is pointed at an object, for example, a menu choice, on the monitor screen in order to make a selection.

LIM-EMS: Abbreviation for Lotus Intel Microsoft Expanded Memory Specification.

Line: A generic term for a transmission medium. It may actually be a line, as in a cable, but increasingly it is likely to be a microwave or optical fibre link.

Line cater: A bug in older versions of Usenet newsreader software for UNIX that caused certain lines at the beginning of posts to vanish. To appease the line cater, posters would include lines of spurious text to be sacrificed instead of the actual contents of the message.

Line feed: A character that moves the cursor down one line (ASCII 10) usually starting a new line in combination with a carriage return character.

Line Graph: A type of graph that links, or attempts to link, all of the data points of a dataset.

Line Length: The number of characters that fit on a line—fixed on some systems, settable on others. The standard, line length on the Internet is 80 characters: e-mail or Usenet posts produced with software using longer line lengths will wrap irregularly and appear awkward to users with 80-character lines.

Line noise: Static or interference on a wire that corrupts the signal. On a character-based modern connection, for example, line noise might result in random gibberish and escape characters polated with the intended text.

line-oriented: (adj) Said of applications and interfaces that display text one line at a time, rather than making an entire screenful of text available at once.

Link: (n) 1. In UNIX, a reference to a directory or file contained elsewhere that appears in directory listings just as if the remote directory or file were in the current, directory; 2. On Web pages, a hypertext connection, a button or high-lighted bit of text that, when selected, jumps the reader to another page.

Linear Programming: A mathematical procedure used to determine the best combination of limited resources and activities necessary to fulfil a specific objective. Although termed "Linear Programming" this technique predates "programming" in its modem sense.

Line Printer: A fast moving printer, used on mainframe and minicomputers only. Line printers are also known as "Line-at-a-time-Printers" as they assemble the characters on a line by line basis, not on a character basis as do most other printers. Output of line printers is often measured in metres of paper per minute or boxes of paper per hour! Types of line printer include a Band Printer, a Chain Printer and a Drum Printer. See separate entries for each of these.

Link Access Protocol (LAP): A data link layer protocol for AppleTalk that specifies the interface to network hardware.

Linker: A software application that links object files, library routines, procedures and variables into a, form ready for execution as a program. Some compilers are also linkers, they take source code and produce an executable file, by passing a separate linking process.

Linotronic: A proprietary brand of typesetting equipment, developed and manufactured by Linotype Corporation. Linotronic typesetters provide very high resolution (1200-2500dpi) and are commonly used at commercial printing premises.

Linux: *(line-ux)* An implementation of UNIX for IBM PC-compatibles. It has been developed as a collaborative effort by widespread Internet users and is distributed for free.

Liquid Crystal Display: This is a type of monitor which uses an alternative to cathode ray technology and is particularly useful where power supplies are limited. A Liquid Crystal Display (abbreviation LCD) uses aromatic hydrocarbons, for example, quinones, which polarize when a voltage is applied to them. This enables the quinones to either pass or block light. Background lighting falling on a LCD screen is normally reflected, however where the quinones allow light to pass through, the image of the appropriate character is formed. LCD technology depends on background lighting, in the absence of this the LCD display is useless. Many manufacturers have overcome this by providing "background" lighting.

LISP: A high level language designed in the late 1950s at Massachusetts Institute of Technology (USA). LISP is used for Artificial Intelligence and other complex applications.

List: (v) 1. To view the names of files in a directory; 2. *To* display the contents of a file.

Listserv: A type of automated mailing list software that runs on IBM mainframes and originated on the BITNET network.

Littleendian: (adj) A storage format in which the most significant byte has the highest address, as opposed to big-endian.

Liveware: People (as opposed to hardware or software)

Local: (adj) Said of a computer to which a user is connected directly or of a device (such as a printer) or process under the user's direct control, as contrasted with remote hosts, devices, and processes.

Local Area Network: A computer network whose participants are located close together often within the same building. Local Area Networks have the advantage that they can utilise very high data transmission speeds and the terminals, which are often personal computers, can share expensive resources such as laser printers and software.

Local Area Transport (LAT): Digital (DEC) architecture for connecting terminal servers on Ethernet networks to host computers.

Local echo: 1. A copy of the data being sent (usually typed) over a communications device (such as a modem) displayed in a terminal window so that the sender can monitor the process; 2. A terminal mode in some communications programs, specifying half duplex transmission, in which the communications program displays the user's input on the screen, instead of relaying an echo from the host.

Localhost: (n) Also local host, the host computer a user is currently logged in to. The *address of* any user's current localhost is always 127.0.0.1.

Local node: The computer on a network to which a user is connected directly.

LocalTalk: Shielded, twistedpair wiring and connectors for using the Macintosh's builtin AppleTalk network hardware.

Local Variable: A variable whose value is controlled by a program module, such as a subroutine. The variable may or may not be accessible to the main program and/or other modules, however only the module containing the "local variable" can alter its value. This is a useful programming technique as it allows compartmentalisation, and therefore safeguarding, of different program variables.

Locative domain name: A twoletter geographical domain name, such as us for the United States, *uk* for the United Kingdom, *de* for Germany, and so on.

LOCIS: The *Library of Congress Information Service,* available by telnet at locis.loc.gov or on the Web at http://www,loc,gov/.

Lock up: (v) To freeze, as when certain sequences of characters, freeze a keyboard, preventing the user from typing.

Log Book: Nautical jargon borrowed by the computer profession. A log book is often used to keep a record of computer staff on duty and the processing tasks performed. It may also be used to keep a record of hardware maintenance schedules and breakdowns.

Logical: Said of a computer address or device, identified by a numerical reference, which may or may not correspond to a physical address or device.

Logic Error A program fault that does not necessarily prevent the program running but produces an output error. Programs with logic errors invariably run through from first to last statement but produce the wrong answer or output.

Logical conjunction: A word that joins two or more key words by specifying a logical relationship between them.

Logical Drive: Part of a physical storage medium (for example, a hard-disk) that has been separated by the operating system into distinct storage locations. The hard disk may have a storage capacity of 42MB, but for operational reasons (users preference or operating system restrictions) it may be necessary to divide the 42MB into two logical drives". Under MS-DOS the two locations may be designated as the C and D drives (A and B are usually reserved for floppy disk drives). In this case the C and D drives share a common physical storage medium.

Logic Gate: A flip-flop, or collection of flip-flops, that will 1 and respond to varying input conditions. Widely used in a CPU and in registers.

Logical Link Control (LLC): The Institute of Electrical and Electronic Engineering 802 standard that specifies a uniform user interface.

Logical tree: Any logical arrangement of devices, files, data, and so on in which all relationships stem from a root; child branches are subordinate to parent branches, and an element without any children is called a leaf.

Logical Unit: Software that communicates with an IBM SNA network.

Log in: (v) To connect to a network or computer, identify oneself as a user, supply a password, and start a session.

Login: (n) 1. A username, the *handle a* user logs in with, corresponding to an account; 2. An instance of logging in.

Login script: A prerecorded sequence of login steps that can play back automatically to connect a user to a computer or network.

Login scripts can breach security if they automate the process of supplying a password, thereby allowing anyone who runs the scıipt to log in.

Log-on: The process of gaining access to computer facilities. This may include entering a password.

Log out: (v) To end a session and disconnect from a computer or network.

Longitudinal Redundancy Check: An error checking technique, used in data communications, in which the parity check character is applied to each column of bits within a data block.

Loopback: (n) A test in which a signal is sent from a source to an intermediate point and 'hen back to the original source to evaluate the accuracy of the transmission.

Loopback address: The Internet address (127.0, 0.1) that always points back to the localhost.

Low-bandwidth: 1. Said of a connection that can only manage a slow connect speed or of a resource on the Internet that a user with a slow connection will still find useful. 2. Colloquially, con dining little useful information.

Low Level Format: The basic installation of a hard disk, usually only performed once in the lifetime of a hard disk.

A low level format is also known as a preformat and can be performed by many disk management utilities.

Low Level Language: A programming language that is fairly close to the machine code used by the processor.

Low level languages are often hardware specific and are not necessarily portable between computers.

LSI: Abbreviation for Large Scale Integration, the manufacture of integrated circuits where many thousands of electronic circuits are placed on one silicon chip.

Lurk: To read a mailing list or newsgroup without posting to it. Every new user should lurk for a while before posting to get a feel for what the group is all about and how others in the group behave.

Lurker: One who lurks. On any mailing list or in any newsgroup, there are usually many times more lurkers than regular contributors.

M

MaasInfo Package: A set of documents written by Robert E. Maas explaining how to use various Internet resources, available via anonymous FTP from aarnet.edu.au in the pub/doc subdirectory.

MAC address: The address that identifies a particular piece of hardware out of several connected to shared media.

MacBinary: A Macintosh file transfer protocol that specifies how files should be transmitted over modems.

Machine Code: A series of on/off signals (binary 0 and 1), the only method of communicating with a processor. The loading of data and instructions into the CPU can only be accomplished by using machine code. Regardless of what type of language (low level or high level) a computer programmer uses, the program must eventually be converted into machine code.

Machine Cycle: The fundamental operating cycle of the CPU, during which the CPU fetches, interprets and executes an instruction word.

Macintosh: A personal computer, based on a Motorola microprocessor, employing a GUI. It was introduced by Apple Corporation in 1984.

Macintosh archive: The largest source of Macintosh shareware and files is the Macintosh archive at Stanford University. Connect via anonymous FTP to sumex-aim.stanford.edu and look in the info-mac directory. This site is also mirrored at the wuarchive.wustl.edu FTP site in the/mirrors/info-mac directory.

Macintoy: A derogatory term for a Macintosh, implying that it is a toy computer, not suitable for hardcore computing.

Macintrash: A derogatory term for a Macintosh.

MacPPP: PPP (Point-to-Protocol) software for the Macintosh, developed by Merit Computer Network and available as freeware via anonymous FTP from ftp.merit. edu in the internet.tool /ppp/mac directory.

Macro: A series of instructions that may be recalled by pressing a single key or entering a simple code. Macros are a mini programming language and are typically used on spreadsheets and word processors.

MacSLIP: SLIP (Serial Line Internet Protocol) software for the. Macintosh, developed by Hyde Park Software,

MacTCP: TCP/IP protocol software for the Macintosh, built into version 7,5 of the Macintosh operating system.

MacWeb: A Web browser for the Macintosh, created by EINET and available via anonymous FTP from ftp.einet. net in the /einet/mac/ macweb directory.

Mac weenie: A pejorative, or affectionate term for a Macintosh aficionado.

Magick: Magic in the sense of the occult, natural or supernatural mysteries, study of the kaballah, and so on, spelled with a *k* to distinguish from stage magic.

Magnetic Core: One of the first forms of computer memory, magnetic core uses windings of copper wire to store magnetic pulses (representing 0 or 1).

Magnetic Disk: A disk that is coated with iron oxide, thereby enabling the introduction (writing), retention (memory) and reading of magnetically recorded informa-tion.

Magnetic Ink Character Recognition: A technology used by many financial institutions. The numbers on a cheque are printed in magnetic ink (ink with a high iron oxide content). For cancellation, the cheques are fed into a Magnetic Ink Character Recognition (abbreviation MICR) reader where the MICR hardware/software identifies the customer who wrote out a particular cheque. All the operator has to do is key in the value of the cheque and the transaction is processed.

Mail: (n) 1. On the Internet, synonymous with e-mail, that is, *electronic mail,* messages carried electronically from computer to computer; 2. The name of a simple UNIX mail program.

(v) 10 send an e-mail message.

Mail address: 1. An Internet e-mail address of the form *username@host.domain;* The *username* portion of a mail account on a network.

Mailbomb: (n) A huge number of messages or an enormous chunk of data, such as a core dump, sent to an e-mail address as a prank or attack on the recipient, in hopes that the bomb will overload or even crash the user's mailer program.

(v) To send or encourage others to send a huge number of messages or an enormous chunk of data.

Mailbot: A *mail server*, a program that automatically responds to mail by sending information or performing functions specified in the incoming mail.

Mailbox: A file, directory, or area of hard disk space used to store e-mail messages,

Mail bridge: A device that connects networks and filters mail between them, passing only messages that meet certain criteria.

Mail-enabled application: A program that, in addition to its normal capabilities, can also handle the sending and receiving of mail.

Mail Exchange Record: A record type in the Domain Name System that identifies the mail-serving host for a given domain.

Mail exploder: A program that forwards an e-mail message to all the addresses on a mailing list.

Mail gateway: A computer that passes e-mail from one network to another, from a network to the Internet, or vice versa, reformatting the headers as necessary.

Mailing list: A discussion group, commonly referred to on the Internet simply as a list, consisting of people with a common interest, all of whom receive all the mail sent, or posted, to the list. Mailing lists are often more specialized than Usenet newsgroups. Lists can be moderated or unmoderated.

Mail Merge: A facility provided on most word processors, where, for example, a predesigned form (a proforma) is merged with a database of customer addresses. The proforma may be a standardised letter, for example, a letter of reminder about outstanding accounts, or a memo, for example, a notice of meeting.

Mail-news gateway: A computer that collects posts from a mailing list and forwards them to a corresponding newsgroup, and vice versa.

Mail path: A list of sites an e-mail message must pass through on the way from the sender to the receiver. Although it is rarely necessary any longer to specify the route your mail will take, mail headers still often include the entire mail *in* back to the sender.

Mail program: Also mail *reader*, the program a user reads, replies to, forwards, and saves mail with. Common UNIX mail programs include mail, elm, and pine. Eudora is a popular mail program for PCs and Macs.

.Mailrc: A setup file for UNIX mail programs (other than elm).

Mail reflector: A mail address that automatically forwards any mail it receives to a list of other addresses.

Mail server: A mailbot, a program that automatically distributes files or information in response to e-mail requests.

Main Distribution Frame: A communications cabling distribution rack, usually located in basement areas of multistory buildings.

Mainframe: A generic name for a large computer installation. A mainframe computer used to be distinguished from other computers, such as PCs, by superior processing speed, but this is not so today. Distinguishing features of mainframe computers are vast amounts of memory, typically several hard disks in the gigabyte range, one or more tape drives, cassettes, several line printers, a separate computer operators' room, a false floor and tight security.

Majordomo: A type of automated mailing list software, similar to listserv.

MAKE.MONEY.FAST: A chain letter still making its rounds on the Net after many years. It's a classic Ponzi/pyramid scheme.

man: The UNIX command that displays the man pages, online documentation for UNIX programs and commands.

MAN: A Metropolitan Area Network, a highspeed (100 Mbps) public network, capable of voice and data transmission over long distances, connecting LANs across a city or campus.

Management Information Base (MIB): A database, on a host, router, or bridge that

Management Information System: A database system that is used to support the management of an organisation, project or resource.

For example, a Management Information System (abbreviation MIS) may be used to assist in the management of an airline, a large building project or a National Park. A MIS is not necessarily an online, working database. It may draw data from the day-to-day activities of the organisation, project or resource but it is generally not involved in actual transaction processing.

Manchester encoding: A method of data-transmission that enables network interface cards to transmit digital signals using direct current, encoding data, and timing signals in the same data stream, as opposed to non-return to zero (NRZ) encoding, which employs two voltage levels—negative and positive—to represent 0 and 1.

Mang: 1. An undefined expletive, uttered or written in response to statements or actions so outrageous or bewildering as to overload a civilized person's ability to respond; 2. The sound the boo tree makes, straining to express the ineffable.

Man pages: The *manual pages*—online documentation for UNIX commands and programs.

Marble Teleconnect: SLIP (Serial Line Internet Protocol) software for the Nextstep operating system, developed by Marble Associates.

Mark as unread: To save a newsgroup article as if it were still unread.

Martian: (adj) Said of a packet that arrives with an incorrect or impossible source address.

MASM: Abbreviation for Macro Assembler, a low level programming language that incorporates the use of macros as a programming tool.

Mass ACK: A message sent to a mailing list requesting a response, in order to test the currency of the addresses on the list.

Mass Storage: A form of secondary storage that uses automated methods of retrieving and loading individual storage devices, for example, cartridges and cassettes. A mass storage system may incorporate an open fronted rack of several hundred cartridges, any of which can be retrieved and loaded automatically.

Massage: (v) To edit, extract, information from, or format a file, as in 'I'll have to massage this data some to figure out what it means.

Match: (n) In a search, a record or document that meets the specified criteria.

Matrix News: A newsletter of the Matrix Information and Directory Services, on the subject of networks, avaible via WAIS at matrix_news.src.

Maximum Transmission Unit (MTU): The greatest datagram length allowed on a particular network.

Maxwell's Demon: Nine-teenth-century Scottish philosopher James Clerk Maxwell postulated that temperature could be regulated in a room by posting a demon at the entrance who would only allow air

Maxwell's Demon: molecules moving at a certain speed or higher to enter. This theory is the probable source for the computer terms daemon and demon

Mb: Abbreviation for megabit.

MB: Abbreviation for megabyte.

MBONE: The *multicast backbone,* an experimental, highspeed virtual network that can send packets simultaneously to a large number of Internet sites, suitable for audio and visual transmission. In 1994, a Rolling Stones concert was multicast to workstations around the world via the MBONE

Mbps: Abbreviation for megabits per second.

MCA: Abbreviation for Micro Channel Architecture. A proprietary (IBM) computer architecture for personal computers.

Mean Time Between Failure: A measure of the elapsed time between equipment failures, usually quoted in the number of operational hours. For example, the Mean Time Between Failure (abbreviation MTBF) of a hard disk may be 20000 hours.

Media Access Control (MAC): The lower component of the data link layer, which defines how computers on a LAN share access to a transmission medium, used in CSMA/CD (Carrier Sense Multiple Access with Collision Detection) and token ring LANs.

Media filter: A device that converts the signal from a token ring adapter board for a particular type of wiring.

Median: The middle value of a dataset. In the following dataset the median value is 4. As there are nineteen items in this dataset the median is the middle value. In the case of an even number of data items, the median is the mean of the two middle items.

Medium: Any substance that conveys a signal from a sender to a receiver, such as copper or other wire, coaxial cable, optical fiber, and so on.

Megabit: One million (2^ 20) bits. This term is often used to describe the memory capacity of RAM chips, for example, "this is a, one megabit chip". Eight one megabit chips would be required to store one megabyte of data, since one byte = 8 bits (on most computers a ninth "parity" bit is added to the data so one megabyte of data would actually require nine one megabit chips). Abbreviation Mb.

Megabits per second: A measurement of transmission speed (such as modern speed or network speed).

Megabyte: This term is used as a measure of the memory capacity of hard disks and tapes. A byte is eights bits (binary digits) of information and is roughly synonymous with one character of data storage (that is, each character stored in memory will take up one byte of storage). A megabyte (abbreviation MB) is 1048576 (2^ 20) bytes.

Megahertz: One megahertz (abbreviation MHz) is one million Hertz (or one million cycles). A signal (sine wave) that completes one cycle once per second is said to have a frequency of one Hertz (also one/ cycle per second). The unit Hertz is a metric unit (named after H R Hertz, 18571894, a German scientist) that replaces cycles per second. MHz is the unit used to measure processor clock speed. For example an Intel 8088 microprocessor based computer may run at 9.5MHz, whereas an 80386 computer may run at 20MHz and often much faster.

Meltdown: What happens when a network is so overloaded that it crashes.

Membrane Keyboard: A keyboard that uses very low profile keys, sealed from the external environment. This type of keyboard is used for computer applications where dust, moisture, hygiene or vandalism may be a problem. Examples of usage include Automatic Teller Machines (ATMs) and industrial control processes.

Meme: (rhymes with *seem,* n) A self-replicating and self perpetuating idea, concept, saying, pun, or way of thinking. For example, how many times have you heard "The Eskimo language has a thousand words for snow" or words to that effect? It doesn't matter that it's not actually true; it is such an infectious or useful metaphor that it sticks in the mind and circulates from person to person perpetually.

The word *meme* was coined as an analogy to *gene* (in the sense of the "selfish" gene that propagates itself, using people as a medium) as well as *phoneme* and *morpheme* (in the sense of a "unit" of thought). The study of memes is called *memetics.* When i powerful set of memes (such as a religious philosophy) is unleashed on the Internet, it is called a *meme plague.*

Memory: A generic term used to describe any data storage area of a computer. Memory may be broadly divided into two types, primary memory, which in most cases requires a power source to retain data; and secondary memory which does not require a power source once the write operation is complete. Primary memory is always located very close to the CPU, often on the same circuit board, whereas secondary memory may be several hundred metres away. Some examples of memory are RAM (primary memory) floppy disks, hard disks, tapes and CDROM (secondary memory).

Memory Chip: A generic name for any form of integrated circuit memory, for example, DIPP, DRAM, FRAM, RAM, SIMM, SRAM.

Memory Management Unit: A part of the CPU or an adjunct to it, which provides specific memory management services. For example, it may provide cache memory management.

Menu: An onscreen display where the computer user can make selections of different programs, software tasks or options. Selections can be made either by highlighting the desired item via the cursor control keys, by using a pointing device, such as a mouse, or by typing the first, or other designated letter of the menu selection.

A selection may be made by highlighting the desired item or by typing the underlined character in combination with another key, for example ALTS. Each menu selection may lead to other menus (submenus) and many software applications, for example, Lotus 1-2-3, have many different levels of menus.

Menu Driven: A computer system or software application that is dependent on commands given by menu selections. In practice most applications use a mixture of direct commands and menu selections.

Message: 1. An e-mail letter; 2. A comment sent to a specific person on IRC and not to the entire channel; 3. A packet.

Message cancel: A feature of some mail programs that allows the user to catch a message and "unsend" it

Message of the day: A message from a network's system administrator that is displayed whenever a user logs in.

Message handling service (MHS): A popular e-mail protocol for storage management, and exchange, especially in corporate offices, licensed by Novell.

Message handling system: The CCITT X.400 protocol for store-and-forward messaging.

Message switching: Also called *packet switching*, a store-and-forward method for routing messages in which each message is passed from a source through intermediate nodes to a destination address.

Message switching: A store-and-forward method for routing messages in which each message is passed from a source through intermediate nodes to a destination address.

Mess-dos: A pejorative term for MS-DOS, impugning its elegance.

MFLOPS: Abbreviation for Millions of Floating Point Operations per second. MFLOPS are used as a measure of processing speed. The present generation of micro-processors are recording processing speeds of 0.1-0.7 MFLOPS.

Metasyntactic variable: A dummy variable, a stand-in variable used in an example to clarify a point of syntax.

MFM: A type of hard disk drive technology which uses Modified Frequency Modulation (MFM) for read/write operations. This is a more efficient method than the older Frequency Modulation techniques and provides higher data transfer rates.

mget: The command in the UNIX ftp program for multiple get, to get a number of files at once.

Microcom Networking Protocol (MNP): An error-checking feature built into many modems. MNP organizes data into frames, then transmits the frames, sometimes compressing the data as well.

Microcomputer: Analogous to personal computer, the term microcomputer is generally only used in educational situations, giving the categories of computers, micro, mini and mainframe. The dividing line between the three categories is by no means clear.

MicroDroid: An employee of Microsoft, especially one who defends the company in Usenet newsgroups.

Microfiche: A film negative, approximately 15cm x 11cm, that is used to record/archive data, for example, stock control records, national library records, meteorological data etc. It requires a special "microfiche reader" in order to be accessed. Microfiche can be produced directly from computer output and is an example of 'hard copy'.

Microfilm: A film negative that is used to archive textual information, for example, newspapers.

Microphone: A communications program for the Macintosh.

Microprocessor: The main brain of most modern computers, providing the fundamental command and instruction environment for the computer. The microprocessor contains a processor, registers, a Control Unit (controls the execution of a program and provides housekeeping functions), a clock and an Arithmetic Logic Unit (performs mathematical operations, comparisons). A microprocessor is contained on a single chip, hence the name "microprocessor".

Microsecond: A unit of time representing one millionth of a second. The symbol for a microsecond is us.

Microsloth Windows: A derogatory term for Microsoft Windows.

Microsoft: An American software developer, founded by Bill Gates and Paul Allen in 1975. Microsoft developed the word's most popular operating system (MSDOS) and many other very successful software applications.

Microsoft Network: An upcoming online service from Microsoft, access to which will come built-in with Windows 95.

Microwave: An ultra high frequency section of the electromagnetic spectrum (of which visible light is just a small part). Microwave is used in many communications applications, such as satellites. One microwave channel can accommodate a vast amount of data/voice/television circuits. Microwave is also used for ground based communications, many communications links that were previously serviced by underground cables now use a series of microwave stations.

Microsoft Windows: A multitasking operating environment that runs on top of MS-DOS and provides IBM PCs and compatibles with a GUI (graphical user interface) not unlike that of the Macintosh, including icons, dialogue boxes, menus, and a mouse pointer.

The upcoming version of Windows, called windows 95, is rumored to include TCP/IP support as well as direct access to Microsoft Network, which itself will include full access to the Internet.

Mid-level network: A regional network, a vague Internet level category between backbone and rib levels.

.mil: An Internet domain corresponding to U.S. military organizations.

Millisecond: A unit of time representing one thousandth of a second.

Hard disk access times are typically measured in milliseconds (abbreviation ms).

MIME: *Multipurpose Internet Mail Extensions,* a protocol that allows e-mail to contain simple text plus colour pictures, video, sound, and binary data. Both the sender and the receiver need MIME-aware mail programs to use it.

Minicomputer: A small mainframe computer, typically used in businesses with less than 100 employees and in small academic institutions. The boundary between a mini and an actual mainframe is blurred.

Minority On-Line Information Service (MOLIS): A service maintained by the U.S. government offering educational and other information, as part of Fedix, available via telnet at fedix.fie.com (log in as *fedix).*

MIPS: Abbreviation for Millions of Instructions per Second. MIPS are used as a measure of processing speed. The present generation of micro-processors are recording processing speeds of 28 MIPS.

Mirror: (v) To store an exact copy of files at another archive site (in order to minimize the load at the original site or provide an archive site geographically closer to some users).

Mirror site: An archive site (generally FTP) containing an exact copy of the files at another site.

Misc: A Usenet hierarchy devoted to whatever doesn't fit in the other hierarchies.

mkdir: The UNIX command to make a directory.

mnemonic: *(ne-mon-ic,* n) A word that helps one remember a command or shortcut. For example, in WordStar (an archaic word processing language), the *cut text* command is Ctrl-Y; the mnemonic to help remember this is *yank* (because you're yanking the text out of the document).

By association, the term has also taken on the meaning of the shortcut or command itself; thus, in the WordStar example, *Ctrl-Y* can also be called the mnemonic for *cut.*

Mode: One of several possible states a program can be in. The most common example of this is the requirement some older text editors such as vi have that the user must first enter insert mode before typing anything.

Modeless editor: A text editor that does not require the user to execute a special command to enter insert mode in order to begin typing. Most new text editors are modeless. On UNIX systems, pico is a modeless editor and vi is not.

Modem: A telecommunications device used to convert digital signals, typically the output from a computer, into a form (analog signals) suitable for transmission over a communications channel (often part of the telephone network). Two modems are required for each channel as the analog signals must be converted back to digital at the receiving end. The name modem comes from the processes involved, modulation demodulation.

Modem bank: A set of shelved modems connected to a host or BBS to allow many callers to log in.

Moderate: (v) To review articles submitted to a list or newsgroup and post only those which meet certain criteria (minimally, they must be on topic).

Moderated: (adj) Said of lists and newsgroups whose posts must pass muster with a moderator before appearing.

Moderator: The volunteer who decides which submissions to a moderated list or newsgroup will be posted.

Modula-2: A high level language devised by Nicholas Wirth. This is an up-dated version of PASCAL which was also devised by Wirth.

Module: 1) Part of a hardware device, usually a plug-in item.

Module: 2) Part of a computer program. Many pro-grammers build up a library of modules which they can call on at any time to form part of many different programs. For example, a programmer may have written a module which uses Newton's Approximation to solve an equation a module that prints out her company logo; a module that monitors the number of hard disk read/write operations. Some or all of these modules can be utilised as and when required by using the appropriate lines of code or compiler directive.

Monitor: A computer peripheral that provides the user with an instant status and update of computer activities. Monitors use similar, but for many reasons different, technology to a television screen. On some "home computers" a monitor is not supplied and the user must plug the computer into a TV set. There are many different monitor technologies in use.

Some of these are:

CGA (Color Graphics Adapter). Low resolution screen, with colour capabilities.

EGA (Enhanced Graphics Adapter). Middle resolution screen with colour capabilities. Introduced by IBM in 1984.

HGC. Hercules Graphics Card. Monochrome output (single colour, often green or amber) with high resolution. Introduced by Hercules Computer Technology in 1982.

MDA. Monochrome Display Adapter. High resolution monochrome screen with a limited number of display lines.

Monochrome. Single colour with high resolution.

Multisync. Capable of a variety of screen and adaptation to different control cards. It also has colour capability.

RGB. Colour monitor that is often used with a CGA card. The initials RGB stand for Red-Green-Blue, a reference to the colours it can display.

VGA (Video Graphics Array). High resolution screen with colour capabilities. VGA uses analog logic whereas most other devices use digital logic. Introduced by IBM in 1987.

Super VGA Uses more pixels (56% more) than VGA Introduced by a group of American companies in 1988.

Some of these names refer to the monitor, some to monitor types and control cards. For example, a dealer may offer a monitor with a CGA/ EGA card.

Monospace font: A font in which all the characters are the same width (as opposed to a proportional-width font, in which the letters *w* and i, for instance vary greatly in width).

For e-mail and newsgroup posts, the 80-character line length standard presupposes a monospace font.

MorF: (written only) Short for *Male or Female* asking about another user's sex.

Morning Star PPP: PPP (Point-to-point Protocol) software for Nextstep, developed by Morning Star Technologies.

Mosaic: The first graphical Web browser, developed by National

Center for Super computing Applications, which greatly popularized the Web in the last few years, and by extension the Internet, as it made the multimedia capabilities of the Net accessible via mouse clicks.

Mosaic exists in freeware and shareware versions for the Macintosh, Windows, and X Window systems and is available via anonymous FTP at ftp.ncsa.uiuc.edu.

Moskvax: One of the sites in the path c: the famous April Fool's kremvax post in 1984.

MOTAS: (written only) A member *of the appropriate sex.* A way of referring to a potential partner without specifying that person's sex.

Motherboard: The main printed circuit board of a computer. The mother-board usually houses the microprocessor, ROM, RAM and many other devices. These items are said to be "on-board". Additional circuitry may be mounted on "daughterboards" which plug into the motherboard.

Motion Picture Experts Group: An ISO committee that proposed the JPEG audio-video compression standard.

MOTOS: (written only) *Member of the opposite sex.*

MOTSS: (written only) *Member of the same sex.*

Motto: A followup post on a newsgroup, proposing the previous post as a motto for the group or for Usenet as a whole, perhaps facetiously.

Mouse: An electromechanical device used as a pointer to select items from an on-screen menu. Mice were originally designed with the idea of reducing the number of key strokes required for a particular task. The most common mouse uses an internal, magnetically coated ball to detect movement of the mouse across a flat surface, usually a desk top. Movement of the mouse is monitored via an input port and this is translated into movement of an icon, usually an arrow, on the screen. Menu selections can be made by pressing one or more buttons on the mouse body when the arrow is located on the required item. Many software applications provide for use of a mouse, but equally as many do not.

Mouse potato: A human being who spends inordinate, chunks of his or her waking life glued to a computer screen, mouse in hand.

Mozilla: A slang name for the Netscape Web browser.

MPEG: A compressed file format for movies.

.mpg: A file extension that indicates MPEG compression.

mput: The command in the UNIX ftp program for *multiple put,* to send a number of files at once.

Multiplexor: A communications device which combines the signals (data) from many different, usually unrelated, sources for transmission purposes. At the receiving end another multiplexor separates the individual signals. Multiplexors provide a convenient means of maximising the rate of usage of a communications channel and are used extensively in all areas of communications.

Multi-tasking: Computer hardware (processor) and software that will permit more than one program to run (actively) at the same time.

Multiple Virtual Storage (MVS): IBM's standard mainframe operating system, similar to VM (Virtual Machine).

Multiplex: (adj) Using a single transmission medium to transmit over multiple logical channels at once, such as when an Internet site maintains HTTP. FTP, SMTP, telnet, and other channels.

Multitasking: (n) The simultaneous execution of two or more programs by a single computer.

N

Nastygram: 1. An e-mail chastisement from a net.god for violating netiquette;. 2. A particularly vicious flame; 3. A letterbomb.

National Information Standards Organization (NISO): A U.S. organization for standards in information, technology, and computing, most specifically as related to the Internet and WAIS, author of the revised WAIS standard.

National Institute for Standards and Technology (NIST): An organization of the U.S. government that promotes national standards of measurement, technology, computing, and networking (formerly the National Bureau of Standards).

National Public Telecommunications Network (NPTN): A nonprofit network that promotes freenets and public networking in general.

National Research and Education Network (NREN): The network established by the High Performance Computing Act of 1991, intended to link government agencies, research organizations, and schools.

National Science Foundation (NSF): The U.S. government agency that funds and runs NSFnet, and consequently many university links to the Internet. Besides its involvement with the Net, NSF promotes science and research.

Natural Language: A programming language that relies on everyday words to generate commands. Whereas most software applications require knowledge of a particular command structure, natural languages (abbreviation NL) let the application user enter commands in a freeform, personal manner. Natural Languages are also called Fifth Generation Language although many computer gurus say that they are Fourth Generation.

Navigate: A computer jargon term meaning to get mound a program, find commands, move through a document, or hunt around the Internet.

Navigator: CompuServe's graphical soft ware for browsing its online service.

Nazis: Mention them, or Hitler specifically, and you've officially ended a thread on Usenet.

ncftp: A sophisticated UNIX FTP program (a cut above ftp) that helps to automate and streamline FTP operations.

NCSA telnet: A free telnet client for Macintosh or Windows, available via anonymous FTP from ftp. ncsa.uiuc.edu.

Near Letter Quality: High resolution output from a printer. Many printers have low and high resolution settings on their control panels. In low resolution settings the print characters are not precisely formed, however for a draft copy this is usually acceptable and saves ink and time. High resolution settings are often labelled NLQ, an abbreviation for "Near Letter Quality". Low resolution settings are often labelled "Draft".net. 1. The original Usenet hierarchical distinction, superseded by the big seven hierarchies (comp., news., misc., rec., sci., soc., and talk.) in the Great Renaming; 2. A prefix added to a lot of common words to suggest their counterparts on the Internet.

net: An Internet domain, corresponding to constituent networks.

Net: *Also net* and *net,* often used as an abbreviation for the Internet or for Usenet, really a more general term for the lump sum of interconnected computers on the planet.

Net.celebrity: Someone famous on the Net (usually meaning on Usenet).

Net.citizen: A responsible member of an online community.

Net.cop: A derogatory term for someone who tries to censor or control the posts of others on Usenet.

NetCruiser Windows: software for CSLIP access to the Internet, distributed by Netcom Online Communication Services (it only connects via Netcom).

Netdead: (adj) Said of someone who has signed off IRC and can no longer be reached.

Netfind: An Internet resource for finding e-mail addresses, reachable by telnet (the exact address depends on where you are).

Nethack: A popular text-adventure dungeon game, similar to Rogue.

Nethead: 1. A Dead Head (fan of the Grateful Dead) who participates in the rec.music. gdead newsgroup (which is gated to the dead-flames mailing list) or any of the many Dead discussion groups on online services; 2. Any obsessed Internet user (a more recent definition of the term).

Net.heavy: A person who knows a lot about how the Internet and Usenet work and whose opinions carry a lot of weight.

Netiquette: Accepted proper behavior on Net. especially in regard to e-mail and Usenet Violate netiquette at your peril. Although the Internet and Usenet are effectively anarchies, they still have strong social cultures, and most of the rules and regulations of the Net are enforced by peer pressure.

Net.kook: Any frequent Usenet poster whose posts reveal a strange and possibly obsessive personality.

Netlag: An excessive delay on IRC that causes messages to bunch up.

Net.legend A net.celebrity: net.kook, or other famous Internet/Usenet figure, many are discussed in the Net.Legends FAQ.

Net.Legends FAQ: A FAQ document that praises and excoriates various net. legends, available via gopher from dixie port 6969.

NetManage Chameleon: TCP/IP software for Windows and DOS.

Netnews: *Also news* another name for Usenet.

Net.personality: A somewhat well-known person on the Net.

Netrc: A setup file for the UNIX ftp and ncftp programs.

Netscape: The state-of-the-art Web browser for Microsoft Windows, Macintosh, and X Window, which, on top of allowing point-and-click Internet access and integration of text, pictures, sound, and movies, also provides security features and the ability to interact with documents before they're fully loaded. It's available for free to individual users via anonymous FTP from ftp. mcom.com.

Netter: Someone who explores the Net.

Network: An interconnection of more than one computer and associated peripheral devices.

Network Database: A database in which the relationship of different data elements to one another is shown in a hierarchical manner but with horizontal links between subordinate entities.

Network address: 1. The unique name of a node on a network; 2. An e-mail address.

Network File System (NFS): Not to be confused with *NSF* the National Science Foundation), a UNIX presentation layer protocol developed by Sun Microsystems that makes it possible for a user to access files elsewhere on the network just as if they on the user's own computer.

Network Information Center (NIC): An organization that provides information and help to users of a network, as the InterNIC does Internet.

Network layer: The third layer of the OSI Model. (IP governs the network layer in the TCP/IP protocol suite.)

Network News Transfer Protocol (NNTP): The protocol used to distribute Usenet newsgroups.

Network operating system (NOS): A set of programs that enables networked computers to share files devices.

Network Operations Center (NOC): An organization that oversees network, monitoring its traffic and solving problems.

Network peripheral: A device, such as a printer, that is directly connected to a network and not to one of the computers or workstations.

Network Time Protocol (NTP): A protocol that synchronizes time information on the Internet.

Newbie: (n) A beginner on the Internet or especially Usenet (not as derogatory as clueless newbie)

Newgroup: A special kind of control message that creates a new newsgroup.

Newgroup wars: Competing newgroup and rmgroup messages repeatedly posted by people, who alternately want and don't want a new newsgroup to be propagated.

The New Hacker's Dictionary: The printedbook version of the jargon file, published by MIT Press and well worth owning in book form. The contents of the jargon file are also available via the Web at http:// www.ccil. org/ jargon/j argon. html.

Newline: Any character or group of characters used to indicate the start of a new line in an ASCII text file. The newline characters vary from system to system. An ASCII file that is mistakenly transmitted as a binary file to an incompatible system can end with garbage characters such as ^M at the end of each line.

News: A Usenet hierarchy devoted to Usenet policy, guidelines, and administrative issues.

Newsfeed: The packet of new's articles passed along from one computer to the next or. Usenet.

Newsfroup: A common typo for newsgroup, now accepted (facetiously) as an alternative spelling.

Newsgroup: A Usenet discussion group.

Newsgroup creation: In the big seven Usenet newsgroup hierarchies, new newsgroups can be created only after a formal RFD (Request for Discussion) and a subsequent CFV. In the alternative newsgroup hierarchies, it is much easier to create a new newsgroup, which accounts for the proliferation of abandoned silly groups.

Newsgroup name: The hierarchical name of a Usenet newsgroup, starting with the firstlevel hierarchical distinction, followed by a dot, then one or more further qualifying names, none of which may be longer than 15 characters, each of which is separated by a dot. In proper newsgroup naming, hyphens or underscores rather than dots should be used to break up compound words, For example, alt.fan.jimj.hendrix is incorrect, but alt.fan.jimi-hendrix is correct.

Newshroup: A common typo for newsgroup which, unlike newsfroup, has not been accepted as a humorous alternative spelling.

.newsrc: A setup file for newsreaders on UNIX systems that keeps track of which Usenet newsgroups the user is subscribed to and which articles have been read.

Newsreader: A program used to read Usenet articles, and usually also to save, respond to, and post follow-ups to articles, as well as to post new articles.

News server: A program or computer that a supplies a newsfeed.

NewsWatcher: A newsreader for the Macintosh, available via anonymous FTP from sumex-aim.stanford.edu.

Newsweeding: A pun on *newsreading,* meaning the process of killing or ignoring uninteresting threads and zeroing in on the worthwhile content of a highvolume newsgroup.

Nexis: An information service of Mead Data giving access to a searchable database of news and magazine articles and abstracts.

Nextstep: An operating system for UNIX hat offers a graphical user interface.

NISO: National Information Standards Organization

Nixpub: A list of Internet service providers, posted, regularly to comp.bbs.misc and alt.bbs, also available via anoymous FTP from vfl.paramax.com in the /pub/ pubnetc: directory.

Nodal Switching System (NSS): The routing method of the NSFnet backbone.

Node: A hardware device that forms part of a computer or data communications network. Each one of these devices is a node.

Non-Breaking Hyphen: This is a term used in word processing, where a hyphenated word should not be split at the end of a line. For example it might be considered confusing to split the phrase "flip-flop" between two lines. The insertion of a nonbreaking hyphen will ensure that the two words are kept together.

NOR Gate: A logic gate that has two or more inputs and one output. A NOR gate detects when either or both inputs are absent, that is if either (or both) input reads 1 then the gate makes no output.

Input A	Input B	Output
0	0	1
0	1	0
1	0	0
1	1	0

Normal Distribution: There is a tendency for all naturally occurring phenomena to clump uniformly around a mean value. Examples include the height of children in a particular grade at school, the length of life of a particular hard disk, the amount of petrol used per year per head of population. This tendency produces what is known as a "Normal Distribution". Graphically a normal distribution produces a characteristic bell-shaped curve.

Norton Index: One of several methods by which computer hardware/ software processing speed may be evaluated. Abbreviation NI.

NOS: Network Operating System.

NOT: [Boolean operator] used to reverse the logical relationship to one of the search elements. A text search for x AND NOT y will match only documents that contain x and do not contain y.

NSTL: Abbreviation for National Software Testing Labora-tory, an American independent software testing and evaluation organisation.

O

Object File: Lines of code that are to be linked into machine code, or into a standalone executable file.

Object-oriented: Said of an operating system, programming language, or application that makes use of selfcontained objects that can contain both programming code and data, and which function as modular program pieces.

Object Oriented Programming: A programming technique that concentrates on the data that is to be processed rather than the means of processing.

Obligatory content: Something added to a mailing list or Usenet post to make it relevant to the charter of the list or newsgroup (replacing the * with the subject of the group, as in obligatory Amiga content or obligatory cat content, and so on).

Obsolescence: Used to describe the premature replacement of products (hardware or software), not because of normal wear and tear or deterioration, but because technological advancements have necessitated their replacement by more uptodate items.

Octet: Eight bits, especially on a system in which eight bits do not equal a byte.

Odd parity: A method of verifying the correctness of transmitted data by summing each byte, adding a parity bit of 1 if necessary to make the sum odd, before sending the data, and then repeating the summation on the receiving end.

OEM: Abbreviation for Original Equipment Manufacturer.

Many hardware devices are manufactured under licence by companies other than the hardware designer, these licencees may quote stock or part numbers which refer back to the OEM (Original Equipment Manufacturer) design specification or part numbers.

Offline: 1. Not currently connected to the Net; 2. Not responding to network requests; 3. Said of a person no longer involved in a chat.

Offfine mail reader: A program that connects to the Net, downloads your e-mail, and then disconnects, allowing you to read, reply to, and send mail without being service charged for connect time.

Offline newsreader: A news-reader that connects to the Net, downloads all unread articles in all subscribed newsgroups, and then disconnects, allowing you to read, reply to, and post articles without being charged for connect time.

Ohnosecond: The elapsed time between giving a wrong command and the realisation that this command will have disastrous consequences. A remarkably short period, of time!

OHP: Abbreviation for Overhead Panel, this is a liquid crystal display that can be connected to a computer (PC) and then placed on an overhead projector for projection on a large screen. A useful teaching/ training aid.

On-Board: A reference to the inclusion of a particular hardware device as part of a "standard" model of computer. An advertisement may state, "1MB RAM on-board" indicating that this amount of RAM is included as standard in this particular model of computer.

One's Complement: The number obtained by changing each bit of a binary number to the opposite value (that is zero become ones and ones become zeros).

On-Line: This phrase describes a hardware device, for example, a printer, that is ready to receive data. A printer can be taken "Off-Line" manually, and automatically if, for example it runs out of paper or toner.

Online Book Initiative (OBI): An organization that publishes uncopyrighted (or no longer copyrighted) books via the Internet, reachable via anonymous FTP at world.std. com.

Online Career Center: A nonprofit, organization that maintains a searchable database of employment information. It offers free access to job listings and resumes to both employers and job-seekers.

Online community: Also *virtual community,* a group of people with shared interests who meet, communicate, and interact via a network, BBS, Internet discussion group, or any other form of electronic common space.

Online Computer Library Center (OCLC): A nonprofit organization providing computer services (such as cataloging and interlibrary loans) for over ten thousand libraries and educational institutions. OCIC maintains the FirstSearch Catalog.

Online service: A company that maintains a proprietary network and provides e-mail, forums, chats, games, databases of information, downloadable files, and information services (stocks, airlines, and so o n) , such as America Online, CompuServe, Delphi, eWorld, GEnie, Prodigy, Microsoft Network, and so on.

Open: To load a file into a software application or into a program. The word "OPEN' is a programming statement in several high level languages.

Open Plan: An office layout where there are few or no internal walls creating separate offices. Instead partitions and office furniture used to create separate work areas.

Open protocol: A protocol that may be utilized by a variey of developers, not just the organization that formulated the protocol.

Open Software Foundation (OSF): An alliance of DEC, IBM, and Hewlett-Packard.

Open Systems Interconnection (OSI): An international organization sponsored by the **ISO** with a mission to create international computer communications standards, such as the OS1 Model, specifically to facilitate internetworking among incompatible systems.

Operating environment: A front end for an operating system, a set of tools and a consistent look and feel that allow the user to interact with the computer.

Operations Research: The development of, and research into, mathematical models for various business and scientific applications. Operations Research is usually computer based. Abbreviation OR.

Operating System: A collection of programs and utilities that provide a basic working environment for other software applications and the computer user. Typically the operating system controls input/output events, memory and file allocation.

Optical Character Recognition: A technology that uses specialised software and pattern recognition to generate a text file in computer memory from printed text. The hardware/software recognises each character, for example, the outline of the letter A, and generates the appropriate ASCII character for input to computer memory. Optical Character Recognition is usually abbreviated to OCR and is also known as scanning.

Optical Disk: This is a generic name for any form of secondary memory that uses optical techniques, rather than solely magnetic techniques, for data storage.

Option: A command or selection available on a menu or list.

Origin: 1) On a graph this term refers to the intersection of the X and Y axis. 2) On a monitor this term refers to the upper left corner. Screen locations are specified in relation to this point. For example the Turbo PASCAL statement GOTOXY(I5,8) would take the cursor across 15 columns and down 8 rows from the upper left corner.

OS/2: An IBM operating system for PCs and compatibles.

Orphan: A term used in typesetting and word processing. An orphan is a small part of a paragraph that appears as the first line at the top of a new page.

OS/2: Abbreviation for Operating System/2. A multitasking operating system developed for IBM PCs using the Intel 80286 and 80386 microprocess tem/2) on IBM manufactured PCs.

OSF: Abbreviation for Open Software Foundation, an American software developers' association.

OSI: *Open Systems Inter-connection,* an international organization sponsored by the ISO with a mission to create international computer communications standards, such as the OSI Model, specifically to facilitate internetworking among incompatible systems.

OSI Model: The seven-layer networking reference model (sometimes called the *seven-layer cake)* defined by the ISO's OSI to facilitate the internetworking of incompatible computers and networks.

Output: Any form of data that is generated by a computer. It may be in the form of on-screen images, printed material or write operations to disk or tape.

Output Device: A generic name for any hardware device that will accept data output from a computer. Examples include printers, monitors, disks etc.

Overflow: The inability of computer memory (RAM) to handle a particular calculation, often caused by pro-gramming logic errors, for example, attempting to divide by zero.

Overhead: (n) The accumulation of protocol information wrapped around data transmitted over networks.

P

Packetized Ensemble Protocol (PEP): A proprietary feature of Telebit brand modems that allows two moderns to be connected directly.

Packet Switching: The transmission of data segments of fixed length so as to improve transmission circuit efficiency. Each data packet may contain unrelated data (data from a variety of sources). However the data packet is transmitted as a complete entity, with the individual data items being separated at the distant end.

Packet sniffer: 1. A person who tries to "listen in" on Internet traffic in search of information to steal; 2. The program that such a person employs to "sniff out" interesting packets.

Packet-switched network: A network made up of interconnected circuits that route packets over a variety of alternative paths, as opposed to a circuit-switched network, in which packets are routed over dedicated lines.

Packet switching: A method of transmitting data in which packets for many unconnected operations are routed simultaneously over a communications channel (often a telephone line) to make best use of the line. Related packets are reassembled at the destination.

Packet switch node (PSN): The computer that the handles the routing of packets in a packet-switched network.

Page: A fixed length data item or program segment that can be loaded into random access memory (RAM) or cache memory as required.

Page Break: A feature of most software applications that Produces text in blocks to suit the designated page (paper) length.

Page Set-up: This refers to how text/graphics will be presented on paper. Attributes of page setup include margins, Orientation, running heads, page numbering etc.

Pagination: In desktop publishing, spreadsheets and word processing, the division of a file into hard copy pages.

PAL: The transmission method used in Australian television. PAL is an abbreviation for Phase Alternate Line, a reference to the changing of colour signal protocol between alternate lines. This technique is designed (with other techniques) to minimise the impact of atmospheric interference. PAL is the most widely used TV transmission technique world-wide, others include the US NTSCT System and the French SECAM System.

Palette: In a graphics package, this is a library of graphics or colours. Palette is a word borrowed from the art world (artist's palette of colours).

Pan: To move sideways from one part of a document or spreadsheet to another, particularly useful where the document/spreadsheet is much wider than the screen display.

Paper Jam: When paper gets tangled up in printer, fax or photocopier hardware. Instruction manuals usually give advice on how to avoid and sort out paper jams.

Parallel Interface: An electrical connection that provides for parallel transmission of data. A parallel interface may also be called a parallel connector.

Parallel Port: An electrical connector that provides for parallel transmission of data.

Parallel Processing: A computer design philosophy that allows a processing task to be split into modules that can be processed in parallel, rather than sequentially, thereby gaining valuable processing time. The high clock speeds of present day microprocessors has meant a vast increase in processing speeds, however many designers are now looking at alternative hardware/software setups to gain even more speed. Parallel processing offers vast gains. The following is an example of "normal" sequential processing.

```
210 A = A + B
220 C = D * E
230 F = SQR(G/H)
240 J = A * C/F
```

Since lines 210, 220 and 230 appear to use unrelated variables there is no reason why these three lines could not be processed simultaneously. All that is required is avoidance of hardware/memory location clashes.

Although parallel processing seems very attractive, continued gains in hardware are producing impressive processing speeds (processors are now being clocked at 80MHz, 50-60MIPS).

Parallel Transmission: A data transmission method where bits (binary digits) are transmitted together, parallel to one another. The alternative to this is serial transmission where bits are transmitted sequentially. Obviously parallel transmission is much faster than serial transmission.

Parameter: A variable or qualifying instruction passed from one program module, procedure or subroutine to another.

Parent directory: 1. In a hierarchical file system, the directory for which the current directory is a subdirectory, symbolized in UNIX, DOS, and OS/2 by two dots (..); 2. Any directory which contains other directories.

Parent Process: A part of a program (process) that generates another subordinate (or child) process.

Parity: An errorchecking method in data transmission in which an extra bit is added to each byte (between the data bit and the stop bit) to round off bittotal values to even or odd numbers. The parity bit must match at both ends of the transmission.

Parity is therefore one of the settings you have to specify on your modem to make a connection. It's usually set to None, or Even, but it depends on the modem calling.

Parity bit: A redundant bit added to a byte in data transmission as part of an error-checking technique.

Parity Checking: This technique is used to detect errors that may occur during data communications and internal data transfers. Parity checking involves adding an extra bit to each byte of binary coded information (for example, ASCII) in order to make the total number of ones (1s) in the byte odd or even. In "even parity" the number of ones is kept even, regardless of the coded information (ASCII character), whereas it is kept odd ill "odd parity". At the receiving end the parity is checked for conformity to 'the agreed pattern, even or odd parity, and any discrepancies attributed to line problems. An error message may be produced or a request generated for a repeat transmission.

For example if ASCII character 'W' (1000001) is being transmitted under even parity then no parity bit would be added since the number of ones is even anyway. If the character "k" (1101011) is being transmitted then a parity bit would be added since there are five ones in the ASCII code.

Parity error: An error caused by mismatched parity bits in a byte of transmitted data.

Parse: (v) To interpret an instruction by breaking it down and analyzing its parts.

Partition: A part of a secondary storage device that is reserved for a particular purpose, either because of user preference or because of operating system restrictions.

PASCAL: A high level language devised by Nicholas Wirth in Switzerland during the early 1970s. PASCAL is a structured language that encourages good programming techniques and is popular in universities and colleges as a teaching tool. There are several proprietary versions of PASCAL on the market, both for mainframe computers, for example, CoPas and VAX PASCAL, and for PCs, for example, Borland Turbo PASCAL, Microsoft Quick Pascal. The following lines are part of a PASCAL program,

```
PROCEDURE OPENFILE(FN STR20; FILESTAT INTEGER);
BEGIN
ASSIGN(F,FN);
IF FILESTAT = 1 THEN
REWRITE (F)
ELSE
RESET (F);
END;
```

Passive star: A network design with a central hub that connects all the branches but does not retransmit signals that pass through it.

Password: A code used to identify a particular user and to control access to particular programs or data files.

passwd: The UNIX command to change an account's password.

Paste: To copy or move part of one file to another part of the same file, or to another file.

Patch: (n) A quick-and-dirty correction that fixes a bug, or at least works around it.

(v) To fix a problem with a temporary work around or kluge.

Patch Panel: A wiring panel with facilities for many different interconnection modes that is typically used for the connection of communications facilities. Connections on a patch panel are usually via jumpers.

Path: A command used, for example, in MS-DOS, to instruct the operating system to look for one or more executable files in one or more directories, other than the present directory.

PC: A *personal computer,* generally a microcomputer, usually either an IBM PC or compatible, a Macintosh, or perhaps an Amiga.

PC-compatible: Said of a computer that emulates the functionality of an IBM PC.

PC-DOS: A proprietary version of MS-DOS used exclusively on IBM PCs.

PC Eudora: A Windows mail program (a port of Eudora for the Macintosh) that PC uses Post Office Protocol and can function as an offline mail reader. It is available via anonymous FTP from ftp.qual comm.com.

PC Gopher for DOS: A gopher client for the IBM PC or compatible running any flavor of DOS, available via anonymous FTP from sunsite. unc.edu.

PC Pursuit: A SprintNet service that allows users to connect directly to another computer.

PC/TCP Plus for DOS DOS: software that enables an IBM PC or compatible to connect via modem to a computer connected to the Internet for FTP and telnet.

PC-Xware: Windows soft-ware that includes TCP/IP, NFS, FTP, and server access for X Window applications, developed by Network Computing Devices. Inc.

PDIAL: *Public Dial Up Internet Access List,* Peter Kaminski's excellent list of Internet service providers, 'complete with cost information, posted regularly to alt.inter-net.access.wanted and alt.bbs.lists, and available via anony-mous FTP from rtfm.mit.edu in the/pub/usenet/ news. answers directory, with the file name pdial.

PDP-11: A series of DEC computers now largely superseded by VAXen. PDP stands for *programmed data pro-cessor.* The PDP-11 series was preceded by PDP-10, accor-ding to hacker lore the first real timesharing machine.

PeaceNet: A BBS for nonprofit organizations, religious organizations, and people concerned with peace and justice. For more information, anonymous FTP to igc.org in the /pub directory.

Peer: A network device that communicates directly with other devices on the network.

Peer-to-peer: (adj) A network architecture in which each computer on the network can communicate directly with other nodes and function as both a client and a server

Pegasus Mail: Also known as *p-mail,* a freeware e-mail program for IBM PCs and compatibles and Macin-toshes, available via FTP from risc.ua.edu.

Peripheral Device: Any hardware that is external to the CPU and its associated hardware. Examples include printers, disk drives, CD-ROM, Bernoulli Boxes, tape drives, scanners, digitizers, code readers, keyboards, mice, visual display units etc.

PENpages: A database and information service covering every imaginable aspect of rural life in general and agriculture in particular, administrated by Pennsylvania State University. It is updated daily and the latest additions are always available on the main menu.

To connect, telnet to psupen.psu.edu and log in as your two-letter state abbreviation (no password).

Pentium: A 64-bit micro-processor, Intel's successor to the 80486 chip (named Pentium after the courts decided that Intel could not defend as a trademark the number 586 or 80586).

The discovery of an error in the muchvaunted chip has spun off a long series of jokes about rounding errors (for example, "Q: How many Pentiums does it take to screw in a lightbulb? A: 1.9999965786.

Peripheral: (adj) Said of a device that is not ess‹ ntial to the computer or physically a part of it (as opposed to the processor or hard-disk drive), such as a printer or modem.

Perl: A programming language (it stands for practical *extraction and report language)* distributed over Usenet, favored by UNIX system administrators.

Permissions: Settings associated with an account on a network or multiuser system that define a level of access (to certain system resources) permitted to the user of the account.

Personal Computer: A microprocessor based computer, commonly abbreviated to PC. The PC was envisaged as a low processing capability "desktop" computer suitable for one person, or a small group of people, to perform fairly routine tasks. The first PCs, then called microcomputers, had very little memory, typically 128KB, and few software applications available to run. Some present day PCs have the processing capabilities, in terms of speed and data storage, of many mainframe computers and the term "Personal Computer" may no longer be appropriate for all "PCs". A typical PC may have 1MB of RAM, two floppy disk drives, a 20MB hard disk and a clock speed of 10MHz. More powerful versions may have 4MB of RAM, two floppy disk drives, a 165MB hard disk and a clock speed of 33MHz.

PERT: Abbreviation for Progress Evaluation and Review Technique. This is a type of flow chart used in manufacturing and service industries to monitor progress of an activity.

PGP: A shareware public-key encryption program (it stands for *pretty good privacy),* developed by Phillip Zimmerman. For more information see the Web page at http:// www. mantis. co. uk/pgp/pgp.html.

Phage: (n) A program that modifies other programs or databases in unauthorized ways.

Phreak: (v) To crack (break into) a network or phone system.

Physical: Said of hardware and mechanical connections, as opposed to logical.

Physical layer: Layer 1 (the bottom layer) of the OSI Model; it defines protocols for connecting cables and other hardware.

Pico: A full-screen, modeless text editor for UNIX machines based on the built-in editor in the pine e-mail program.

Pie Chart: A type of chart (graph) that arranges data in a circular fashion so that the contribution of each data item to the combined data can be visually appreciated. For example a pie chart could be used to show the variation iii product sales throughout the year. Each data item is represented by a "slice" of the pie. An exploding pie chart is where one or more slices of the pie are staggered out from the regular alignment. This is often done to draw attention to one or more data items.

Pile-on: (n) A flame war in which many participants take turns attacking a single victim, creating long posts of polymorphous abuse.

Pin: 1) Abbreviation for Personal Identification* Number. These are used by customers of various financial institutions in conjunction with a credit/debit card to confirm authorised use of the card.

Pine: A UNIX e-mail program whose name is a recursive acronym (pine stands for *pine is* not elm). Pine has a built-in full-screen, modeless editor, MIME support, and the ability to attach files.

.pinerc: *(dot-pine-are-see)* A setup file for pine.

Ping: (v) 1. To check the presence of a host with PING; 2. To send e-mail to an entire mailing list, requesting a response, in order to check which addresses are still valid.

PING: Said to stand for *Packet Internet* a protocol for sending a signal to Whether another network host or other device is online and responding. (It's probably actually named for the sound made by submarine sonar/depth equipment.)

Pipe: (v) To send the output of a process or dump the contents of a file to a device, program, or another file.

Pipeline: A string of commands entered as a group but separated by the software application and/or operating system into individual commands/parameters.

Pipeline for Windows: Windows front end software for a connection to a service provider, developed by Pipeline.

.pit: The file extension for Macintosh PackIt files. (PackIt has largely been superseded as a Macintosh compression standard by Stufflt.)

Pitch: A measure of the size of a printer font. Some software applications refer to pitch sizes, other to point sizes. The majority of the text in this book is set in an 11 point font. To convert point to pitch, divide the pitch into 120, for example, 12 point = 120/12 = 10 pitch.

Pixel: A short form for "picture element". The resolution of a computer monitor is measured in pixels, giving an indication of how well formed the characters will be on the screen. A low density of pixels means poorly defined characters which are very tiring on human eyes, whereas a high density of pixels produces clear character outlines. A very high resolution monitor will have a pixel count of about 1000 x

850, horizontal x vertical. High resolution monitors would have about 900 x 500. Pixels are also used in satellite technology, one pixel of satellite imagery typically covers 50m x 50m on the ground.

.pkg: The file extension for an Applelink Package file.

pkunzip: The uncompression program for pkzipped files.

pkzip: A DOS file compression program.

Plain ASCII: Said of an ASCII text file (a document with no word-processor formatting).

PL/1: Abbreviation for Programming Language 1. This is 5 a very powerful, high level language developed by IBM during the early 1960s.

.plan: A text file that is displayed when your username is fingered. Originally intended to alert people to your whereabouts or immediate plans, .plan files have evolved into personalized files sometimes filled with information or absurdities.

Platen: The roller of a dot matrix printer or typewriter. The platen is only engaged when single sheets of paper are used. Continuous form paper uses sprocket holes which engage in a tractor feed and will not run smoothly if the platen is engaged.

Platter: A flat circular medium, coated with magnetic material that can be used for the storage of data.

Plotter: A computer peripheral that uses pens to generate images. A plotter usually has a flat bed and an array of different coloured pens in a clip rack. The plotter arm, which is under software control, selects the appropriate pen and draws the appropriate images. Plotters are used extensively for drafting and cartography as they provide an exceptionally neat product. On a flat bed plotter the plotter arm provides all of the pen transportation. On a drum plotter the paper is clipped to a rotating drum. The pen is then positioned by the combined movement of drum and pen.,

Platform: A computer operating system type.

Plokta: *Press lots of keys to abort.* Many newbie posts end with a pathetic series of attempts to a quit while still in insert mode, like so:

***Plonk*:** A follow-up post that means I just put you in my kill file."

p-mail: 1. Pegasus Mail; 2. Physical mail, as opposed to e-mail.

POH: Abbreviation for "Power On Hours", a reference to the number of hours an item of hardware, for example, a hard disk, has actually been in use. The Mean Time Between Failure of an item is usually measured in POH.

Point: A measure of the size of a printer font, with one point being approximately 1172.27 inches, 0.351 millimetres. Some software applications refer to point sizes, others to pitch sizes. The majority of the text in this book is set in an 11 point font. To convert pitch to point, divide the pitch into 120, for example, 10 pitch = 120/10 point = 12. The greater the point size the greater the size of the font, inversely for pitch which is a measure of how many characters can be printed per linear inch.

Point at: To start a client program, such as a Web browser, by supplying it with an address, as in "Point your Web browser at http://enterzone. berkeley.edu/enterzone. html to see the latest episode of Entorzone."

Point of presence (POP): A local phone number connected to a modem connected to the network of a service provider, to enable users to log in to the network without paying long distance charges.

Point of Sale Terminal: A computer peripheral that provides on-site input of items sold and immediate debiting of the customer's account. These terminals are common in retail outlets and are very useful for stock control. Abbreviation POS.

Point-to-Point Protocol (PPP): A TCP/IP protocol, similar to SLIP, for transmitting IP datagrams over serial lines such as phone lines. With PPP, PC users can connect to the Internet and still function in their native environment.

Poll: (v) 1. To check a port to see whether a device is connected and available for network or communications activity; 2. To connect to another system to check for new mail or news.

Polling: A design philosophy where the CPU constantly cheeks each device to see if it needs processing time. If not, then the CPU continues polling other devices. Polling requires very fast and constant scanning of each and every device.

Port: Any connector on a computer that provides for data exchange to or from a peripheral device or data comm-unications line. For example, a serial port provides for serial transmission of data, possibly to a modem, a parallel port provides for parallel transmission, possibly to a printer.

Portable Computer: A personal computer specifically designed to be carried by one person and to be used in informal settings.

Portrait: Reference to the orientation of hard copy images. Portrait indicates that the job was printed across the short side of the page, as in this book. The term portrait is derived from the art world, where portraits are usually orientated vertically.

Post: (v) 1. To send a message to a mailing list or an article to a newsgroup;

2. To publish information in any medium on the Internet. (The word *post* comes from the bulletinboard metaphor, in which scraps of paper are posted to the board to be read by anyone who comes by, as opposed to the British usage, which means to send mail.)

(n) A message sent to a mailing list or newsgroup.

Postcardware: Shareware that's almost free, except the programmer requests that satisfied users send a postcard

Postmaster: A person who oversees a network's e-mail connection to the internet. Questions about users at a host or problems with e-mail to or from that host can often be addressed to postmasuer@host name. dimain.

Post Office Protocol (POP): A protocol that specifies how a personal computer can connect to a mail server on the Internet and download e-mail.

Postscript: A powerful printer command language developed by Adobe Systems (USA). Postscript, is used extensively on laser printers and provides very accurate control of the print image.

Pot.Kettle. Black: A shorthand newsgroup or mailing list follow-up, criticizing the previous poster for exhibiting the same foibles she was faulting another for. (It's short for the aphorism "That's like the pot calling the kettle black.")

Pour: (v) To pipe the output from a process or file to a device or other file.

Power cycling: Turning the hardware off, waiting, and then turning it on again.

PPP: *Point-to-Point Protocol*, a TCP/IP protocol similar to SLIP for transmitting IP datagrams over serial lines such as phone lines. With PPP, PC users can connect to, the Internet and still function in their native environment (instead of having to deal with a character-based UNIX environment).

Precision: This refers to the exactness of results and should not to be confused with accuracy. For example, the conversion factor of kilometres to miles may be stated as 1.61km = 1 mile, however it would be more precise to use 1.609km = 1 mile. The use of a more precise conversion factor does not necessarily mean a more accurate answer since there may be mistakes in the program logic, or human error in usage.

Presentation layer: Layer 6 of the OSI Model, it defines how data is formed, encoded, converted, and presented.

Presentation Manager: The on-screen user Interface for personal computers using the OS/2 and PS/2 operating systems. Presentation Manager provides an enhanced environment for the computer user, and simplifies many repetitive tasks.

Primary Data: This is data that is acquired from its original source. Examples of primary data include rainfall data gathered by the Bureau of Meteorology; demographic statistics gathered by the Australian Bureau of Statistics; production data from a vehicle manufacturer.

Primary Memory: This is computer memory (RAM) that is directly associated with the CPU. It is usually volatile, that is, it does not retain memory capability without power. On a byte for dollar basis primary memory is expensive in comparison to secondary memory.

Prime time: The period of heaviest usage of a network, usually 9-to-5 the work week.

Principia Discordia: An underground track that elucidates the worship of Eris, ancient goddess of discord.

Printed Circuit Board: A generic name for any circuit board that has its circuitry "printed" on the surface of the board. Printing is achieved by a photochemical process and lends itself to automated manufacturing. Most, if not all, modern electronic circuits are designed to be manufactured using printed circuit methods. Printing may be on one or both sides of the circuit board, and in some cases may run horizontally through the core of the board. The board is generally made of fibreglass which is used for its ease of manufacture, strength and electrical resistance. Abbreviation PCB.

Printer: A hardware device that produces text or graphics output. Printers are grouped broadly into either, impact printers (dot matrix, chain, drum, daisy wheel) or nonimpact printers (ink-jet, thermal, laser).

Printer Access Protocol (PAP): The AppleTalk protocol that defines how a workstation and a printer communicate.

Printer Driver: A command file that forms part of many software applications, for example, word processors, spreadsheets etc. A printer driver converts standardised commands from the software application into commands that are specific to the printer. Printer drivers are necessary as most printers use a different command structure. The more sophisticated the printer and the print mode the larger the printer driver file. For optimum results it is necessary to load the correct printer driver.

Printhead: This is the mechanism, on a dot matrix, ink-jet printer, thermal printer etc., that actually creates the image on the print media. The printhead usually moves wildly from one side of the print medium to another.

Print Medium: The surface on which a printed image will be generated.. In most cases the print medium will be paper but may also be transparencies, microfiche etc.

Printout: Any hard copy produced as output from a software application.

Privacy: Because the Internet is not inherently secure, users are cautioned to e-mail and post only information that they don't mind being public, or take steps to increase the privacy of their communication, either via encryption, through anonymity, or by using other communications channels entirely.

Privacy-enhanced mail (PEM): E-mail-handling systems that incorporate encryption techniques to secure privacy and verification of message integrity.

Private key: In public-key encryption, the secret key the user reveals to no one and uses to sign outgoing messages and to decrypt incoming messages that were encrypted with the public key.

Private Line: A data communications line, or telephone, video line etc, that is leased from a common carrier and generally used exclusively by the lessee. Synonymous with Leased Line.

Private virtual circuit (PVC): Software circuits that maintain a private line between hosts.

Privatization: On the Internet, generally refers to the U.S. government's process of placing maintenance of backbone networks in the hands of private organizations. So far this has not significantly changed the pricing structure for individual users.

Privilages: Also called access privileges, a set of system resource and directory actions that a user is permitted to perform.

Problem Solving: This is the six step process of identifying the problem, gathering and sorting relevant information, developing and analysing alternatives, programming, implementing the program and following up. The ease with which problems are solved is largely a matter of experience, coupled with the use of appropriate problem solving techniques.

Procedure: A module of a PASCAL program. Use of arguments (parameter passing) allows a procedure to perform programming tasks on similar, but not necessarily identical datasets. The following lines of code are an example of the usage of procedures,

```
BEGIN
CHKSTR('EMPLOYEE - Surname ? ',SNAME,10,17);
CHKSTR('EMPLOYEE Initials ? ',FNAME,10,19);
CHKREAL('PAY RATE - $',SAI,10,21);
CHKINT('POSTCODE- ',PCODE,10,23);
END;
```

The Procedure CHKSTR is used twice in this example, controlling screen output and keyboard input for two different data items, an employee's surname and initials, merely by passing different parameters to the same procedure. The main body of a well written PASCAL program is likely to be just a listing of all the procedure calls, the procedures having been declared and coded in the program header.

Process: A program or part of a program being executed in a multitasking operating system. More generally, one task of many that a computer is doing.

Processor: A generic name for any processor or micro-processor. Processors provide the fundamental control structure for any computer. The processor recognises commands, received in machine code, and generates the necessary machine code in response to the instruction.

The instruction may be a simple task such as getting data from memory or a series of extensive calculations. The name "Central Processing Unit" (CPU) is sometimes used interchangeably with "processor", however a CPU contains more than just a processor. The name microprocessor is sometimes applied to small, 8-bit or less, processors, however micro-processor is more correctly applied to any "processor on a chip" such as the Intel 80286, Motorola 68000 etc.

Processor Control: Any device that uses a processor for its fundamental, centralised control, is said to have processor control or to be processor controlled (also microprocessor controlled). Examples include telephone systems and many industrial processes, for example, glass making.

ProComm Plus: A popular communications package for IBM PCs and compatibles, sold by Datastorm Technologies.

Program: A series of instructions written by a computer programmer or operator for execution by the computer user. Programs are executable files, that is, they do something tangible with computer hardware (and possibly other software).

Program Counter: A register, located within the CPU, which is used to hold the address of the next executable instruction. To begin executing any program the program counter has to be set to the address of the first instruction. The processor always starts by fetching the opcode and then decoding the opcode to determine what to do next. It is the opcode that tells the processor whether or not it has to fetch an operand address before it can execute the instruction.

Program Header: The lines of code which introduce all the variables, arrays, procedures, library modules etc to be used in a program.

.project: On some systems, a file similar to a plan that is displayed when a user is fingered, intended to discuss the project the user is currently working on.

Project Gutenberg: An organization that publishes uncopyrighted books on the Internet, reachable via anonymous FTP at mrcnext.cso. uiuc.edu.

PROLOG: Acronym for PROgramming LOGic. This is a high level language used mainly for writing Expert Systems and artificial intelligence programs. It was developed in England and France during the early 1970s.

PROM: Abbreviation for Programmable Read Only Memory. This type of Read Only Memory (ROM) can only be programmed once.

Prompt: An on-screen character used to indicate that the computer is ready to receive the next command, sometimes called a "system prompt". Prompts vary from one operating system to another and according to user preferences. They often use an alphabetic character in combination with a graphics character.

Propagation: The process of dissemination for packets in general, and Usenet newsfeeds in particular, as they are passed from computer to computer. Propagation delays are responsible for the sometimes confusing situation that occurs when you read a follow-up to a post that hasn't yet appeared at your site.

Proportionally Spaced Font: A design of font that allocates variable linear space to each different character as it is letter "w" would be given more space than the letter "i". In comparison a fixed space, or "fixed font", always allocates the same linear space regardless of which character is being printed.. Use of proportional spacing gives a much more professional appearance to text. Most word processors can specify proportional spacing (proportionally spaced fonts) but not all printers can produce the necessary output.

Proprietary: Said of a technology, architecture, or set of protocols whose design is the property of the company that developed it.

Prospero: A distributed directory system, file system, and index service (and the protocol that underlies it) that allows users to access both local and remote directories in the same way. For more information, connect via anonymous FTP to prospero.isi. edu and go to the /pub/ prospero directory.

Protocol: A list of established or agreed "rules". Protocol is often used in data communications to specify Baud Rate, Parity Checking etc.

Protocol layer: One portion of a set of protocols that handles one aspect of the transmission of data.

Protocol stack: A set of protocol layers that work together to provide reliable communication between a computer and a network or another computer, also called a Protocol family or protocol suite.

.ps: The file extension for PostScript files.

Pseudo: (n) A new identity assumed on Usenet in order that the user might act (provocatively or otherwise) without those actions being associated with the user's real name.

/pub: A UNIX directory often found on FTP hosts, where public information is stored and made available.

public data network (PDN): A type of commercial packet-switched network offering wide-area services to customers, with sophisticated errorchecking, buffering, and handling of *protocols.* Tymnet, Sprint Net, and the CompuServe Packet Network are all PDNs.

Public domain: (adj) Available for free to the public, un-copyrighted, as are much of the information, system software, and applications available on the Internet.

Public Domain Software: Software that has been developed either by software enthusiasts or commercial software developers and made freely available to the public. Commercial software developers may place software in the Public Domain if they are trying to promote a particular concept or industry standard.

Public key: In publickey encryption, the key a user distributes freely and which correspondents use to encrypt messages to the user and decrypt the user's signature (encrypted with the user's private key) on messages from the user.

Public-key encryption: A form of key encryption which uses two keys, a public key and a private key to enable users to verify each other's messages without having to securely exchange secret keys.

Q

Query: (n) 1. A search request submitted to a database to find a particular record (piece of information) or all records that meet certain criteria, such as an archie query; 2. A question mark.

Question mark: 1. A wildcard character in UNIX (and hence in many Internet applications), it stands for any single character., 2. A help command in some character-based applications.

Questionnaires: Usenet newsgroups are often bombarded by purveyors of questionnaires hoping to exploit a ready made audience.

That the responders are selfselecting doesn't seem to bother the questioneers, but to regular readers of the newsgroups, these posts and the ubiquitous surveys get tiresome awfully fast.

Queue: *(cue,* n) A list of items (such as print jobs or messages) waiting to be sent from one device to another.

QuickTime: An Apple technology that debuted with Macintosh System 7. It compresses, Stores, and plays back files combining text, sound, animation, and video, Many QuickTime clips are distributed via the Internet and the Web.

Quit: To stop running an application and (usually) return to the operating system.

Quoting: Including a relevant portion of a preceding article when posting a followup.

Most newsreaders precede quoted text with a symbol, such as >, and try to indicate who said what, though multiple embedded quotations often require that the latest author untangle the attributions.

It is bad netiquette to quote no text (unless the followup makes it absolutely clear what it is responding to), and it's both bad netiquette and an unmistakable marker of a clueless newbie to quote an entire article merely to add "I agree" or "Right on, dOOd" at the end.

R

RAM: *Random access memory*, memory that any application or process can read or write to. It's frequently confused with storage, because both resources are often measured in megabytes.

Ranking: The order in which a WAIS program displays the results of a database search—from most likely to least likely.

rc file: A UNIX text file with a file name of the form, *rc, containing command line instructions or other startup information for an application or for the operating system itself. Examples include newsrc, pinerc, and so on.

README file: An information file describing the contents of an FIT directory or the files associated with an application.

Readme.txt: Typical name for a README file.

Read notification: A feature of some e-mail programs that lets you know when the recipient of your e-mail has received and opened the message.

Read-only: (adj) Said of a file that can be read but not altered.

Read-write: (adj) Said of a file that can be both read and written to (altered).

Real life: The offline world, as in the question "What do you do in real life".

Real name: Also called a full name, a user's full name as it appears on e-mail messages and Usenet posts., as opposed to their username (the real name can also be a pseudonym). On UNIX systems, the user's real name is a variable that can be set with the chfn command. Many Windows and Macintosh Internet applications allow the user to enter or change a real name on the fly.

Real Soon Now: Also *RSN,* similar to *as soon as possible* but with a subtext that it ain't really gonna happen any time soon.

Real time: Also *realtime,* the time used for synchronous communication, in which both participants must be available. Also, taking place at me present time, live, not delayed or recorded.

Reboot: To restart a crashed operating system, either through a designated key combination (a warm boot), or by turning it off and on again (power cycling).

Rec: A Usenet hierarchy devoted *to* recreation.

Receipt notification: A proof of delivery feature provided by sonic e-mail programs (similar to the idea of registered mail in the real world).

Record: (n) A set of related data from a database.

Recursive acronym: An acronym that contains the acronym itself in its spelled out form, such as GNU, which stands for *GNU's not UNIX,* and pine, which stands for pine is not elm.

Redirection: Sending output from one device or file to another device or file.

Refresh: To redraw the screen, usually either to reflect changes to the data or to restore the screen when something has marred its intended appearance.

Redundant path: A secondary path that a router can assign to a packet when the normal route is not available.

Register: (v) To sign up and pay for shareware.

(n) A designated area of memory.

Registered jack (RJ): Any of a series of specialized jacks used for connecting wires, such as RJ-11 and RJ-45.

Rehi: *(ree-high) Hi again,* typed on IRC when you rejoin a channel.

Relevance feedback: A system used by WAIS applications to rank documents retrieved in a search in order of relevance to the search criteria. Documents are ranked based on the number of times that key words from the query appear in them.

Reliable: Said of networks with dedicated connections.

Religious issues: Neverending debates (such as those that go on in some of the talk. newsgroups) on subjects such as abortion, gun control, or IBM PC vs. Mac.

Remailer: A program that receives e-mail and then resends it, with different information attached.

Remote: Said of a host or other network resource that is locate d on a computer or network elsewhere, as opposed to a local host or resource.

Remote access: The process of accessing another computer's resources, such as files or printers. Dial-up accounts and telnet are both forms of remote access.

Remote login: To connect to a remote computer over a network, usually done on the Internet with telnet or rlogin.

Remove: To kill or erase a file or directory.

Rename: To change the name (or path) of a file or directory.

Repeater: A device that connects two stretches of cable and boosts the power of the signal it passes, to reduce line noise and the risk of errors.

Reply: (v) To respond to an e-mail message or Usenet post.

(n) 1. A message sent in response to a previous message or post; 2. An e-mail command that takes the return path from the current message and makes that address the recipient of a new message, possibly quoting the previous message as well.

Repost: (n) An article posted again in full. (Many newsgroups expect that reposts be labeled as such in their subject lines.)

(v) To post the same information again.

Request for Discussion (RFD): The first stage in the formal process of Usenet newsgroup creation.

Request: A suffix appended to the user name of a human-administered mailing list to form the username of the administrative address for the list. (So a human administered mailing list called atoz@ netcom.com would have an administrative address called atoz-request@ netcom.com associated with it.) It is a Bad Thing to post administrative requests (generally to subscribe or unsubscribe) to the actual mailing list rather than to the request address.

Research Libraries Information Network (RLIN): An online catalog of catalogs with information from most major research libraries in the United States, reachable by telnet at rlg.stanford. edu (it's not free).

Reseaux Associes pour la Recherche Europeenne (RARE): A European group of research networks. For more information, connect via anonymous FTP to ftp.rare.nl.

Reseaux IP Europeenne (RIPE): A group of European TCP/IP networks.

Resolution: 1. Conversion of a physical address into a logical address *(address resolution);* 2. The degree of detail, sharpness, or fineness of an image.

Resolve: (v) To convert a physical address to a logical address or vice versa.

Return from the dead: (v) To be reconnected to the Internet after a hiatus.

return path: An address in the header of an e-mail program that tells the recipient's mail program where to send a reply message.

Reverse Address Resolution Protocol (RARP): A TCP/IP protocol for converting logical addresses to physical addresses.

RFC: *Request for Comments,* one of a set of documents that contain Internet protocols, standards, and information, and together more or less define the Internet, in ai) open way. The standards contained in them ire followed carefully by software developers The name Request for Comments can be confusing, since the contents are settled, but they arrived from free and open discussion on the Net.

RFCs can be found via anonymous FTP at the ftp.internic.net site, among others.

rib site: A computer with a high-speed link to a backbone site that distributes traffic to smaller networks.

rights: Another name for privileges.

Right Thing: Something which is absolutely, the right thing to do.

ring topology: A network architecture in which the nodes are arranged in a circle.

RINGO: An experimental service at MIT that allows you to rate a list of musicians and bands and receive back some suggestions about other music you might like.

RJ-45: A modular jack that can hold up to four pairs of wires, used most often to connect unshielded twisted-pair wiring in LANs. An RJ-45 looks like a phone jack (Rj 11) except bigger.

rlogin: A protocol (and program) for remote login from one UNIX machine to another. It automatically supplies the username and password given when the user first logged in.

rm: The UNIX *remove* command, for deleting a file.

rmdir: The UNIX *remove directory* command, for deleting a directory.

rmgroup: A special kind of control message that removes a newsgroup.

rn: The most common UNIX newsreader. It's not a threaded newsreader.

robocancel: (v) To automatically cancel articles. A controversial (because it's a form of censorship) method for dealing with spammers and roboposters.

robopost: (v) To post automatically, usually done by a 'bot that is programmed to post reams of articles and responses to Usenet.

roboposter: 1. A 'bot that automatically posts and reposts huge numbers of articles to Usenet.

robot: A user on IRC or in a MUD (or, less commonly, on Usenet) that is actually a program. Some perform useful functions while others are merely annoying:

Robust: Said of software that doesn't crash often and recovers well when it does.

Rogue: A widely circulated text-adventure role-playing game, with a dungeon/ swords-and-sorcery motif.

role-playing game: A game or activity, such as a MUD, in which participants take on fictional identities and strive to remain in character.

ROM: (rhymes with prom) *Read-only memory.* Fixed memory that can't be altered.

root: (n) In a hierchical file system, the first directory, to which all other directories are sub directories.

rot13: *(rot-thirteen)* A simple cipher in which each letter is replaced with the one 13 letters away from it in the alphabet, traditionally used to hide spoilers and offcolor jokes from sensitive eyes.

S

Scalable Font: A soft font that can have its point size changed after its data file is created.

Scanner: A peripheral device that converts a printed image into digital information suitable for input to a computer. Some scanners, the more expensive models, will convert text into an ASCII file, others treat text as a graphic. A flat-bed scanner uses a flat surface, similar to that found in a photocopier, whereas a drum scanner requires the image, which is usually paper, to be fed into a series of rollers.

Scatter Plot: This is a type of graph which can be used to show the approximate correlation, if any, between two sets of data. It is called a scatter plot since the data points are placed (scattered) as individual dots across the graph, their actual positions being determined by the parameters of the graph.

Scientific Notation: A method of representing large numbers by using a two part notation. For example, the number 13000000000 can be represented by using a stem, also called a radix, and a corresponding "power of ten" multiplier, also called an exponent. In the example given, this number could be represented as 0. 13 x 10 ^ 11 or 1300 x 10 ^ 7. Scientific notation is often used by high level languages to provide convenient output of an otherwise lengthy number. It is also used on calculators where there is a limited amount of output display area. Using the above example, the onscreen display of a scientific notation number takes the format 0.13Ell, where E is the power of ten multiplier. In some programming languages (for example, C) program variables can be declared as being "floating point". Some languages use the name "double precision" as an alternative. Variables should only be declared as floating point if absolutely necessary as these numbers will have a large amount of RAM (for example, 8 bytes) allocated to them.

Scratch File: A temporary file set up during the execution of a program.

Scroll: To move the onscreen image. This usually only refers to vertical movement, horizontal movement is usually called "panning", but may be called horizontal scrolling.

SCSI: Abbreviation for Small Computer Systems Interface. This is a secondary storage interface that provides a high data transfer rate (typically 4MB/sec) and up to seven storage devices accessible via the one control card. SCSI (pronounced scuzzy) is used on many PCs.

Search: A facility found in most word processors and in some programming environments. The search facility allows the user to specify that each occurrence of a word or part of a word or group of words be located by the software.

Search and Replace: A facility found in most word processors and in some programming environments. This facility allows the user to specify that each occurrence of a word or part of a word or group of words be replaced with another group of characters, or words etc.

Seasonally Adjusted: A phrase use to describe a dataset that has been adjusted to allow for seasonal factors (fluctuations) that may hide or modify previous trends. Seasonally adjusted data gives a more reliable and accurate picture of the situation. Secondary Data. This is data that has already been collected for another purpose and is now being used as a data source. Examples may include information extracted from a journal article or a newspaper story.

Secondary Memory: A generic name used for any nonvolatile mass storage medium. Memory may be broadly divided into two types, primary memory, which usually requires a power source to retain data, and secondary memory which does not require a power source once the write operation is complete. Primary memory is always located very close to the CPU, often on the same circuit board, whereas secondary memory may be several hundred metres away.

Second Generation Computer: This phrase refers to those computers developed during the period 19551965 *using* transistor technology, but *only* as discrete components. Integrated circuits formed the Third Generation.

Sector: A subdivision of a hard disk or floppy disk. Sectors are generally pieshaped, getting wider as the edge of the disk is reached. A typical floppy disk has 10 sectors, a hard disk, 17.

Seek Time: The amount of time taken for the read/write head to get to the required track.

Selenium: A semiconductor material, similar in properties to silicon, however its switching speed is slower than silicon.

Semiconductor: A generic name for any silicon, germanium or selenium based electronic device. These three elements are found in the Periodic Table of Elements at the juncture of metals and nonmetals and are conductors under certain electrical conditions, nonconductors under others, hence the name semiconductor.

Sequential Access: A method of data storage in which each data entry is stored in a sequential manner, one after the other. A computer tape is an example of a sequential storage medium as is a home video tape. The main disadvantage with sequential access is that to get to say, the 900th data record, the tape must be wound through records 1899, a very time consuming process.

Access time is therefore very dependent on where the wanted data item is on the tape, that is whether it is at the beginning or end of the tape.

Serial Port: A connector that provides for serial transmission of data.

Serial Transmission: A data transmission method where each bit of information is transmitted one after another.

Setup: 1) The process of getting hardware or software ready for operation. Generally synonymous with the verb "to install".

Setup: 2) This phrase describes the hardware/software configuration at a particular computer site. Programmers and operators may say "what's the setup here?"

Sferics: This is jargon for "atmospherics", and refers to any form of interference on a communications line. Sferics is pronounced as written.

Shadow RAM: An area of RAM used to take over functions that would normally be handled by ROM chips. Since RAM is faster than ROM this provides improved processing times and better control.

Shareware: Software developed by members of the public and distributed at no cost or for a nominal fee. The onscreen documentation for some Shareware will often request a donation to the software writer.

Shell: 1) This word is usually synonymous with operating system. Many software developers say that their operating system provides the "shell" within which other software applications can operate.

Shell: 2) A command used in some programming languages to temporarily relinquish runtime control by a program in favour of an operating system command. It is said that control reverts to the operating system shell.

Shift Key: A key on a computer keyboard that provides access to upper case letters and the "second function" of all other keys, for example, the key $/4 produces $ when the shift key is pressed, the key %/5 produces % etc. Compare this to the Caps Lock key which only affects the alphabetic characters. The Shift key is usually engraved as "Shift" but often has a vertical arrow symbol (Ý).

Shift Register: This is a register, consisting of a series of interconnected flipflops, which stores binary codes (bits). A shift register allows bits to be shifted 'to the "left" or 64 right". As the binary, and decimal, numbering scheme uses positional notation a move to the right is tantamount ' to division by two, to the left is multiplication by two. In the decimal system a move to the right is tantamount to division by 10. Shift Registers are used by the processor for binary arithmetic.

Side Effect: A step in a program that inadvertently alters the value of data or data Files.

Side effects are hard to find as they are not always apparent to the user, however they can be very damaging.

Signal: A generic name for any information being transmitted or received via a data communications link.

Sign Magnitude Representation: A common technique used to denote negative and positive numbers within the binary numbering system.

The leftmost digit position is used to indicate negative or positive values.

Silicon: A Group 4 element on the boundary between metals and nonmetals. Silicon is a semiconductor and is widely used in the manufacture of electronic devices, for example, transistors, because of its electrical properties. Silicon is recovered from beach sands and occasionally from river gravels.

Silicon Chip: This is an electronic device, manufactured as an integrated structure, that contains many thousands, sometimes hundreds of thousands, of individual electronic components and circuits.

A silicon chip is also known as a chip or integrated circuit. The Intel 486 microprocessor chip contains 1.2 million transistors.

Silicon Valley: An industrial area in California, sonamed because of its high density of electronic industries, all of which use a large amount of silicon, in the area. Its rivals, in terms of number of industries, include Silicon Forest, Oregon.

SIMM: Abbreviation for Single in-Line Memory Module, a type of RAM chip. SIMMs are commonly used to provide RAM in a computer and generally plug directly into the motherboard, they do not require an additional circuit board.

Simplex: A data transmission method which is strictly oneway, data can go in one direction only. Television is an example of simplex transmission, the viewer cannot use the television set to communicate with the TV station.

Single Precision Number: A floating point number that is usually only allocated 4 bytes of memory.

SIPP: Abbreviation for Single in-Line Pin Profile. A RAM chip that has its electrical connections (pins) on one side only.

Site Licence: A licence issued by a software developer, or their agent, authorising the use of particular software on the purchaser's premises. The site licence may authorise the' use of a software application on some but not all machines at the premises.

Smart Terminal: A computer terminal that has a keyboard, a monitor and its own processing capabilities. In a Local Area Network, which uses PCs as the terminal equipment, the terminals are "smart", that is they have their own processor. The phrase smart terminal is also applied to data communications equipment. In this case smart terminals have some limited processing capability.

Snow: Patterns of white dots flickering across a monitor screen. This is usually caused by slight incompatibility between software and monitor.

Soft Copy: Any computer output that does not produce a permanent or visual record. Examples includes output to it monitor, to RAM or to a disk or tape. Origin of name, "soft" implies easily changed.

Soft Font: A font that can be derived on demand from software instructions rather than from hardware, such as font cartridges. Soft fonts are usually cheaper to buy than cartridges, on a font per dollar basis, and are more adaptable to the user's particular requirements. They are usually created during a one-off "manufacturing" session, after which they are stored on disk ready for use. Soft fonts need to be down-loaded to the printer before they can be used and take up valuable printer RAM once down-loaded. Most up-to-date word processors and desktop publishing packages include the ability to download soft fonts, making it a very easy task.

Soft Sectored Disk: A disk whose sectors have been allocated by software progression from a reference point. Hard sectored disks have their sectors allocated by hardware markers. Most disks use soft sectoring.

Software: A set of instructions that direct the computer (CPU) to perform a particular set of tasks in a particular order, using specified hardware devices, memory locations etc.

Software Application: A generic name for any software or computer program.

Software Developer: Any company or individual that designs, codes and markets software products.

Software Licence: This usually entitles the purchaser of a software application to use that application for their own use on one machine only. A licence is purchased as part of a software package.

Software Life Cycle: The processes involved in the development and improvement of a software application.

Software Package: An item of commercial software sold with support material, for example, written and onscreen documentation, as well as access to specialist advisers.

Solid State: Jargon for integrated circuit and transistor based technology.

Source: In a file copy/archive task, the source file is the rile that is to be copied/archived.

Source File: A program, usually written in a high level language, that is being used to generate an object file, either by a translator or compiler.

Spacing: A reference to the dispersion of characters within a word, words within a line or lines within a page of text. Word processors can usually control all or some of these attributes, more finely tuned control is offered by desktop publishing packages.

Spaghetti Code: This is a name given to any program that is written in such a way that it is hard to follow the logic of the program. Spaghetti Code is difficult to follow since there are so many loose ends. Programs with an excessive amount of GOTO statements are a classic example of Spaghetti Code.

SPARC: 1) Abbreviation for Standards Planning and Requirements Committee (of ANSI). An industry committee involved in the development of many different standards.

SPARC: 2) Abbreviation for Scalable Processor Architecture. A form of Reduced Instruction Set Computing (RISC).

Spell Check: A feature of most word processors which provides a thorough, but not infallible, check of the spelling of text files. The dictionaries accompanying the Spell Check facility often do not include all the words that the user is likely to come across. However some word processors allow the user to generate their own dictionaries.

Spooling: A technique often used in a busy work environment to control the flow of work to a limited supply of printers, for example in a network situation.

Spooling software and RAM provides for queueing of each print job on a FIFO basis. Some software applications have their own inbuilt spooling capabilities.

Although very useful when there are multiple users of limited resources, in a standalone PC, spooling operations consume substantial computing time as a large number of operations are necessary to get the file into and out of the spooler allocated RAM or disk space.

To overcome this many spoolers, work in the background. The name spooling is used since its philosophy of operation implies that each job is stored sequentially, much like the negatives on a spool of photographic film. Spool is also an abbreviation for Simultaneous Peripheral Operation OnLine.

Spreadsheet: A mainframe or PC based worksheet providing many rows and columns for numerical data entry. Spreadsheets are widely used in the accounting, scientific and business communities. Typical uses are financial records, scientific analysis and database tasks. The essence of a spreadsheet is the ability to embed formulae amongst the rows and columns of numeric data. Each data entry point, the intersection of row and column, is shown as a cell.

SRAM: Abbreviation for Static RAM. This is Random Access Memory (RAM) that does not lose its data storage capability when power is turned off.

Stack: An area of RAM used as a Last-in First-out (LIFO) data store.

Standalone Computer: A computer designed to be self-contained, not requiring access to any other hardware or software in order to operate satisfactorily. A personal computer is generally a standalone computer.

Standalone program: A computer program that does not need any other software, other than an operating system, to run. Programs that are not standalone usually require the prior loading of other software or access to a software library of routines.

Most commercial software applications use standalone programs. Under many operating systems, standalone programs have the file extension .exe, for example, WP.VXE may be a word processing program, INV.EXE may be an invoice system.

Standard Deviation: A measure of the dispersion of data items within a dataset. If the data has a normal distribution then it is acknowledged that 68% of all data will fall within plus/minus one STDEV, 95% within plus/minus two STDEVs and 99% within three STDEVs.

Star Network: A computer network where the communications links to each computer radiate out from a central computer creating a "star" structure.

State of the Art: A phrase used to describe computer hardware and software, particularly hardware, that is up-to-date, using the latest technology. Increasingly, the terms "State of the Art" and "up-to-date" are more and more difficult to define as the pace of technological advancement increases.

Static Memory: This is computer memory that does not lose its stored data after the power has been turned off. Examples of static memory include floppy disks, hard disks and magnetic tapes.

Statistics: The science of measuring the occurrence, distribution and dispersion of data, numeric or otherwise. Computers are increasingly used for statistical analysis and many software applications have been designed specifically for statistics. Examples include SPSS, Minitab and

Systat. Most spreadsheet packages also provide useful statistics capabilities.

Status Message: A message, that is usually visual, given by hardware devices on their current operating condition. In the case of a printer, such messages may include "Ready", "Out of Paper", "Toner Low", "On-Line" etc.

Stepper: A euphemism for a "conventional" Hard Disk Drive. A stepper provides access to each data storage track by moving the read/write head in discrete steps over each track, hence the name "stepper".

ST506: A type of hard disk controller, commonly used in IBM and IBM compatible PCs. The ST506 controller, uses MFM or RLL and was one of the first disk controllers.

Stored Program Control: A computer philosophy con-ceptualised and developed by John von Neumann (pronounced Noymann), one of the great names of modern technology. Working in the USA, Von Neumann realised that the computers in use at the time were specific task oriented and therefore inflexible.

Streaming Tape: A magnetic tape, used for archive purposes, which stores a non-working copy of all source files.

String: A set of characters. String variables are frequently used in programming for the input and processing of text and alphanumerics. A string variable can record any form of input, numbers and/or text.

Stroke Weight: A measure of printed character density, light, medium, dark etc. This term is jargon used by font designers.

Structured Program: A program that uses modularising techniques to keep the code in manageable, logical sections.

Structured Walk-through: A technique used by pro-grammers and systems analysts, where a person discusses the concepts, design and data flow of a program, or computer system, with another programmer or analyst.

Style: A generic name for the type of lettering used for printer output. Styles may include italic, reverse, shadow, outline etc.

Style Manual: A publication produced by several organisations which sets out the rules and conventions to be followed when editing and producing any sort of publication. It provides a guide to the best typographical and printing practices and is an invaluable reference for people who produce material for publication.

Style Sheet: A part of a software application that allows predesignated paragraph and/or font attributes to be applied to all or part of a text file. Style sheets are found in some word processors, for example, Microsoft Word, WordPerfect, and in desktop publishing packages, for example, PageMaker. A style sheet includes information on paragraph attributes (width, indents, text flow etc) as well as character attributes. Use of a style sheet enables quick and consistent formatting of a document. They are popular with corporate users and publishing houses as they ensure uniformity of presentation.

SubDirectory: This is a directory that forms a subsection of another directory. For example it may be necessary to have a directory "WA" which is used to store all of the information relating to an organisation's WA operations. Subdirectories WA\Payroll, WA\Sales, WA\Assets may be necessary as further categories of the WA directory. These directories, WA\Payroll etc, are known as subdirectories.

SubRoutine: A program module that can be used many times within the same program. For example it may be necessary to find the factorial of a number at several points within a program. Rather than write the lines of code for each occurrence of this need, a subroutine can be called each time.

Subscript: 1) A number and/or letter used to identify an item of an array or matrix. Example, numrec(y), A(10).

Subscript: 2) A character inserted slightly below the text baseline to indicate an ongoing reference, .

Supercomputer: A specialised computer with superior processing capability and vast memory. Such a computer is used where there is a very large dataset to process and for scientific research. There are not many of these machines in Australia, a supercomputer is used by the Bureau of Meteorology, at its Head Office in Melbourne, for weather forecasting and analysis.

Superscript: This is the opposite to subscript. The qualifying character in this case is inserted slightly above the other characters.

Surface Mount Technology: A design technique used in the manufacture and assembly of motherboards, which provides improved layout options through the reduced use of connector pins.

Surge Suppressor: An electronic device fitted to many computer power sources to prevent spikes and surges within the power supply from damaging the sensitive electronic circuitry of the computer. Spikes and surges may be generated by large power consuming equipment such as lift motors, welding devices, compressors etc.

Swapping: A memory management technique used where the program or data file is large and there is a limited amount of RAM. Programs, program segments and/or data are swapped into and out of RAM from secondary storage as and when required, preferably just before being required.

Symbol Set: A set of characters grouped together by font designers because of their specialised usage. For example there may be a mathematics symbol set, an engineering set, a finance set etc. Symbol sets are not often part of the normal character set of a word processor or desktop publishing package, symbol sets usually have to be purchased as a font cartridge or as soft fonts.

Synchronous Transmission: A transmission technique whereby the transmitting and receiving hardware are synchronised from a common clock source or via a rigourously accurate clock at each end.

Syntax: The rules, set down by a software developer, for writing program code. In PASCAL, syntax would include rules such as; finish most lines of code with a semicolon, enclose all comments within asterisks and brackets, match most BEGIN and END statements etc. Syntax errors are detected by the software application during actual coding or during compilation. In either case the syntax errors must be corrected before an executable file can be created.

Syntax Diagram: A flowchart that displays the syntax rules of a particular software application, typically used in programming languages.

System: 1) A generic name for a computer installation, for example, "We have a Hewlett Packard computer system".

System: 2) A command used in some software applications to return the user to the operating system, either permanently or temporarily.

System Disk: A floppy disk that has boot information (system files) on it. This disk can be used to boot a system.

Systems Analysis: The investigation of user requirements for computing facilities. Systems Analysis includes investigation as to how a computer can help increase productivity etc. The specialist personnel involved in this process are usually from a consulting organisation and are called Systems Analysts.

Systems Application Architecture. Proprietary (IBM) specifications for hardware/software compatibility.

Systems Development Life Cycle: The processes involved in the development and improvement of a computer system. Typically the Systems Development Life Cycle (abbreviation SDLC) has seven steps,

— Original Requirements (identifying problems and highlighting opportunities for improvement)

— Determining System and Information Requirements

— Program and System Design (flowcharts, pseudo code)

— Testing, Debugging and Documentation

— Installation and Training

— Evaluation (New Requirements)

Some Systems Analysis professionals say that there are only five steps in the SDLC, others say there are seven steps, however all agree there is a circular process involved and that it may be called a SDLC.

Systems Network Architecture: An IBM design of architecture for computer networks. Abbreviation SNA.

T

Tab: An indent from the left margin of a block of text. The ability to indent text, at user defined steps, is provided as a feature of most word processors.

Table of services: A service provider's internal list of Internet services (such as FTP, finger, IRC, and so on) offered to users.

Talk: (n) 1. One-to-one synchronous chatting over the Net;

2. The UNIX command for initiating or accepting a talk request (the form of the command is talk *username@ address).*

Talk: A Usenet hierarchy devoted to discussion, argument, and debate.

Talk mode: A UNIX feature in which two or more users can participate in an online conversation in real time.

TANSTAAFL: (written only, also tanstaafl) *There ain't no such thing as a free lunch,* of ten pointed to as a general principal of the universe, probably taken from economist Milton Friedman's book *There's No Such Thing as Free Lunch.*

Tape: Plastic tape, usually made of mylar, that is coated with iron oxide, thereby enabling the introduction (writing), retention (memory) and reading of magnetically recorded information. The absence or presence of magnetism is interpreted during read operations as a binary 0 or 1. Tape is more formally known as magnetic tape and is sensitive to environmental conditions (humidity and temperature) as well as external magnetic fields and needs to be stored carefully. It is used in reel-to-reel tapes, cartridges and cassettes.

Tape Backup Unit: A type of secondary storage that uses either cassette or cartridge to backup the contents of a hard disk, these are normally streaming tapes. Abbreviation TBU.

Tape Drive: An electro-mechanical device that loads and moves a magnetic tape in accordance with operator and/or processor demands. A key aspect of the complex mechanism of a tape drive is the ability to maintain a regular speed past the read/write heads. This requires the use of vacuum chambers at the tape entry/exit points.

Tape Leader: This is the first few metres of a magnetic tape. These are not used for data storage since the likelihood of physical damage is high.

Tape tree: A distributing mechanism for audio cassette tapes employed in some of the music-related newsgroups and mailing lists, in which a seed tape is copied by a root participant for a number of branches, each of which, in turn, dub copies for their children on the tree, until copies of the tapes reach leaf participants, who have parents but no children in the tree structure.

Tar: (n) A UNIX program (tape archiver) that concatenates a number of files into a single file (without compressing them). (v) To create an archive file with the tar program.

.tar A file extension indicating that the file is a tarred file, an archive consisting of several concatenated files.

Tar file: A file containing several files, concatenated with the UNIX tar program.

Target: In a file copy task, the target is the disk, directory or tape that will receive the copied file.

.tar.Z: A file extension indicating that the file is tarred and compressed with the UNIX compress program.

Task: 1) A job given to a computer operator, for example, updating payroll files on tape, making a backup copy of a file etc. 2) An instruction, or set of instructions, given to a computer via a batch file or a program.

TCP: Transmission Control Protocol, part of the TCP/IP stack. It functions on the transport layer of the OSI Model, establishing and verifying the data connection.

TCP Connect/II: A suite of Macintosh software com-prising Internet tools such as e-mail, a Usenet newsreader, FTP, and telnet, developed by InterCon Systems Incorporated.

TCP/IP: Abbreviation for Transmission Control Procedure/Internet

Proto-col. This is a network implementation developed by the US Department of Defense. It has many commercial users.

TECO: A once popular text editor with a powerful built-in programming language, now largely supplanted by emacs.

Telecommunications: A general term relating to the transfer of information, such as data, voice and video, over a distance.

Teledildonics: A trendy term for online sex, alluding to the mechanical "interface" devices that might evolve in the near future.

Telemetry: The remote measuring of data, either for immediate transfer to a central data entry site or for later inclusion into a dataset. Examples include river gauging stations, weather stations and traffic measuring devices.

Template: A proforma device, which may be mechanical or software, that enables a uniform product (for example, a text document) to be produced each time the template is used. See also Style Sheet.

Telenet: The original name of SprintNet

Telex: An international communications system made up of linked terminals that can send and receive data. Some online services offer telex access.

Telnet: 1. A terminal-emulation protocol (defined in RFC 854) for remote login over the Internet, part of the TCP/IP suite;

2. The UNIX program that uses that protocol.

(v) To log in to a remote computer via the telnet protocol.

10BaseF: The Ethernet specification (802.3 standard) for fiber-optic cable. (10 for the 10 Mbps bandwidth, *base* for baseband, and E for fiber-optic.)

10Base5: The Ethernet specification (802.3 standard' using "thick" coaxial cable. (10 for 10 Mbps bandwidth, *base* for baseband, and 5 for 500-meter-long cable segments.)

10BaseT: The Ethernet specification (802.3 standard) using two pairs of unshielded twisted-pair (UTP) wire. (10 for 10 Mbps bandwidth, *base* for baseband, and *T* for twisted-pair cable.)

10Base2: The Ethernet specification (802.3 standard) using "thin" coaxial cable (A") also known as *thinnet, or cheapernet.*

Terabyte: One million megabytes (2 ^ 40 Bytes). Abbreviation TB. See also Byte, Megabyte.

Term: A DOS program that enables a personal computer to function as a UNIX terminal-emulation pro-gram over a dial-up connection.

Terminal: A computer keyboard/monitor connected to mainframe computer, for example, as part of an airline reservation system. Also any device connected to a data communications network.

Terminal Access Controller (TAC): A device that provides and maintains a dial-up terminal connection to the Internet.

Terminal emulation: Behaving like a specific type of terminal (such as a DEC VT100 or VT52 or an IBM 3270), passing keyboard input to a computer and displaying computer output on the screen

Terminal-emulation program: Software a personal computer uses to imitate a specific type of terminal (such as a VT100, ANSI, or TTY terminal) and connect to a host.

Terminal/host computing: The model of computing used by dumb terminals and host computers, in which the terminal is only a messenger and the host does all of the processing.

Terminal server: A device that enables several modems (usually assembled on a modem bank) or terminals to connect to a host on one channel by sending a combined signal.

Terminal window: A window in a graphical user interface in which a terminal-emulation program displays an terminal screen connected by network to a remote computer.

Terminator: A device connected to the end of a LAN cable to prevent signals from being transmitted.

.test: Any of the newsgroups with names such as misc.test, alt.test, rec.test, and so on, designated for test posts. If you post to a '.test newsgroup, daemon's all over the Internet send you e-mail acknowledg-ments when your post reaches It is a breach of netiquette to post test messages to any newsgroup other than *.test newsgroups.

One trap often set for newbies is a post with its follow-up line set to a *.test newsgroup. Anyone who responds to the post without noticing and removing the *.test group will suffer a mailbox flooded by well-meaning daemons.

Test post: A post with no meaningful content, posted to a newsgroup (preferably a *.test newsgroup) so that the user can determine if her newsreader software and Internet connection are working properly.

Text editor: An application for editing text files, usually less fully featured than a word processor. The Notepad accessory in Windows is a text editor, as are the UNIX programs vi, pico, emacs, ee, and joe, among others.

Text file: Also *ASCII file* or ASCII *text file,* a file containing only ASCII characters. This means no formatting—no bold or italics, no headers, footers, margin adjustments, non-breaking hyphens, and so on.

Text file transfer: A form of file transfer, both with FTP and with uploading/downloading programs (kermit, zmodem, etc.) used to transfer files containing only ASCII characters. (Newline characters are automatically converted for the operating system being transferred to.)

Text transfer: 1. A text file transfer; 2. A transfer of text directly from a local file to a remote computer, as if typed directly from the keyboard, or from the output of a remote program running on a remote host computer to the terminal window and/or to a text file on the local computer.

T4: A long-distance, digital, point-to-point communi-cations circuit developed by AT&T that transmits a signal at 274.176 Mbps, with up to 168 T1 channels (4,032 channels of 64 Kbps), handling both voice and data.

TFTP: *Trivial File Transfer Protocol,* a simplified version of FTP that does not include password protection.

Thanks in advance: Often abbreviated *TIA* or more whimsically as aTdHvAa Nn KcSe, a common sign-off for requests made on the Internet.

The Internet Adapter (TIA) : A UNIX, program that enables a dial-up shell account to emulate a SLIP connection, allowing the user to run Internet software native to his desktop environment without the full costs (or full functionality, either) of real SLIP. TIA is available from Cyberspace Develop-ment at http://market place.com/.

Thermal Printer: A printer that uses thermal techniques to transfer an image onto a print medium. Most fax machines use thermal techniques. Some thermal printers require special paper, however the IBM Quietwriter is an example of a thermal printer that does not require special paper.

Thomas: U.S. Congressional archives on the Web, administered by the Library of Congress, named for Thomas Jefferson, at http://thomas.loc.cov/.)

Thesaurus: A feature of most word processors which allows the user to find alternative words for a particular, and possibly overworked, word. A thesaurus is an invaluable reference when preparing written material of any kind as it offers a choice of words and phrases to fit any given context.

Third Generation Computer: This refers to a computer developed in the period 1965-1980, using LSI (Large Scale Integration) as the basis of the microprocessor, memory and control. See also First Generation Computer, Fourth Genera-tion Computer, Genera-tion, Second Generation Computer, LSI.

Third Generation Language: This is the present generation of high level languages, examples include BASIC, C and PASCAL. Abbreviation 3GL.

Thread: (n) 1. A series of messages related to the same topic in a discussion group, such as an original post and related follow-ups. It is appropriate to read an entire thread before contributing to it to avoid repeating something that may already have been contributed one or more times; 2. A process that is part of a larger process or program.

Threaded newsreader: A newsreader that organizes posts according to thread and allows you to read your way up or down a thread, such as trn, tin, and Newswatcher.

Throughput: A measure of the amount of work or data that passes through a computer system each working day, week or month. Throughput may be gauged with reference to any chosen measure of performance.

Thwap: A virtual slap, as on IRC, indicating that you've just smacked the recipient for writing something stupid or inappropriate.

TIA: 1. An abbreviation for thanks in advance; 2. The Internet Adapter, a SLIP-emulation program for UNIX.

TidBITS: A weekly newsletter about the Internet and Macintosh computers, distributed via e-mail by Adam Engst.

Tidy: Cool, stylish, and confident, from the idea of structured, well-organized and easy-to-read programming code.

TIFF: Abbreviation for Tagged Image File Format. This is a dynamic graphics file format developed by Aldus and Microsoft in America. Files using TIFF format usually have the file extension TIF, for example, LOG TIF, COVER.TIF etc.

Tilde: The ASCII character number 126 (~). Used in some macro programming languages for example, Lotus 123, to represent a line return (pressing the Enter key). See also ASCII.

Tilde escape: A command in the UNIX mail program that starts with a tilde character (~) and performs a function, rather than inserting text into the mail.

Tune to Live (TTL): An IP packet header field that tells how long the packet should be held before it's purged,

Time out: (v) To fail, as a network process, because the remote server or computer has not responded in time, to close a connection after waiting too long for ack-nowledgment.

Time Division: A transmission technique used to enhance the transmission capabilities of a communications channel. It is also known as Pulse Code Modulation (PCM). In time division each data connection, within a specified group, is allocated a time slot during which that connection transmits or receives data. It then remains silent until its next allocated time slot comes round, in the meantime the other data connections transmit/receive. This means that one physical communications link can be used simultaneously by any different and unrelated users.

Time Division is a form of multiplexing and is commonly known as Time Division Multiplexing (TDM). TDM re quires tight control over each time slot and fast electronic circuitry, which presents no difficulty for modern day hardware. MM was developed during the 1960s, primarily for voice communication (telephone) but is widely used in data communications. In voice communication approxima-tely time slots per second are allocated to each connection. Typically there are 3248 connections per group, giving 25600038400 time slots per second. See also Multiplexor.

Time Series: A long term aggregation of data that may be taken as indicative of the generalised behaviour of the data set, even though the dataset may not be completely known and/or whose future values are not known.

Time Series Analysis: A statistical method used to determine the reasons for long term behaviour of a dataset. For example, the price of wheat rises and falls throughout the year and from year to year. Time series analysis may determine patterns within this rise and fall, identifying seasonality, trends and cyclic events such as drought.

Time Sharing: A technique used on larger computers where several users, or tasks, may share the hardware and software resources of a common installation.

Timeout: (n) The occasion when a remote computer times out.

Tin: A threaded newsreader for UNIX.

TLA: (written only) *Three-letter acronym,* many of which persist throughout the Internet.

tn3270: A program similar to telnet that emulates a 3270 terminal connected to an IBM mainframe.

Toaster: A mildly pejorative name for a Macintosh or PC.

Toggle: (n) A logical or physical switch (or even a single bit) that can be set to two positions, usually on and off. A light switch is a toggle.

(v) To change a switch or bit from one state to the other (from 0 to 1 or back again).

Token Passing: A technique use to prevent more than one user occupying a communications channel. The token is a coded digit that occurs only once throughout the communications system. *The* holder of the token, held in RAM, is the one and only computer able to transmit or receive data. The concept of token passing is borrowed from railway signalling where tokens or batons are carried up and down single track lines so as to (theoretically) prevent train collisions.

Token Ring: A proprietary (IBM) computer network protocol developed in the early 1980s. Ibis protocol is defined in the IEEE 802.5 standard.

Token ring: A (typically IBM) type of network architecture in which nodes are connected in a closed circle. The nodes continually pass a token (a special message) around the circle. To transmit data, a node has to wait until it's "it." Then the data rides along with the token and gets off at the, right stop.

TokenTalk: An Apple product that, enables AppleTalk protocols to work on a token ring network,

T1: A longdistance, digital, point-to-point communi-cations circuit, developed by AT&T, that transmits a DS1 signal at 1.544 Mbps, with 24 (voice) channels of 64 Kbps. If the circuit uses fewer than 24 channels, it's called ET1 or *fractional T1.*

Tool: A utility program, a useful program that performs a set function.

Toner: A dry powder "ink" used in laser printers. Toner is often contained in a hermetically sealed unit known as a "toner cartridge".

Top-Down Design: A method used in Systems Analysis where the overall objectives of the organisation are considered and the fine detail, such as the computer system necessary to help achieve those objectives, is considered from an overall, that is, organisational, point of view. The opposite of Top-Down Design is Bottom-Up, also known as ad hoe.

Topic drift: As threads wear on in discussion groups, they frequently stray from the original topic as listed in the Subject header. Some posters take the initiative of changing the Subject line to spawn new threads.

This same phenomenon is noticed in e-mail conversations, in which the original header, perhaps preceded by *Re: Re: Re:* outlasts its relevance.

Topic group: Any electronic common space for people who share an interest.

Topology: Any type of physical network layout, organizing the devices and the cables connecting them. Most LANs have bus topology, star topology, or ring topology.

Touch Screen: A computer screen which allows the user to select the item (task) they want by touching the screen at the appropriate spot.

Tower: A generic name for personal computers that use a freestanding floor mounted cabinet. Such a design is intended to save desk space. The monitor and keyboard obviously remain on the desk top.

Toy A computer or system less powerful than the one used by the speaker, not necessarily derogatory.

Tpi. Abbreviation for tracks per inch. This is sometimes given as a measure of data density on a floppy disk. For example, there may be 96tpi on a DSHD (1.2MB) 5.25" floppy disk, 135tpi on a DSDD (720KB) 3.5" floppy disk.

Track: This term is used to refer to data storage locations on a floppy or hard disk that although using different sectors, describe a constant radius circle around the spindle. A track may also be described as "all those data storage locations that can be accessed without physically moving the read/write head". A "cylinder" is a collection of identical tracks on a hard disk, or a double sided floppy disk.

Trackball: A hand operated pointing device, used with PCs. Basically a trackball is a mouse lying on its back. See also Mouse.

Tractor Feed: An electro-mechanical device, which is part of a printer, that transports continuous form paper past the print mechanism. The tractor feed has sprockets which engage in the paper, thereby providing traction.

Traditional newsgroup hierarchy: The seven newsgroup hierar-chies in Usenet news proper: comp., misc., news., rec., sci., soc., and talk. New newsgroups in any of the traditional hierarchies can only be created after a formal process, including a request for discussion and a call for votes.

Traffic: The volume of flow in a data communications network, often measured in erlangs. One erlang indicates the occupancy of one circuit for one hour. If a data channel is occupied for 12 minutes every hour then it is said to carry 0.2 erlangs (12/60 erlangs) of traffic.

Trailer: Information follow-ing the data in a packet, signifying the end of the data and possibly including error-checking information.

Transaction: A generic name for any business dealing that would normally include the exchange of information, goods, paper or money.

Transceiver: A device that both transmits and receives signals, exchanging frames between a node and a network.

Transistor: An electronic component that is the fundamental building block of all processors. The transistor was "discovered" by scientists at Bell Telephone Company (USA) in 1948. The name transistor is a combination of transfer-resistor, since it was found that this newly discovered device could transfer a voltage from a low resistance circuit to a high resistance one, and therefore was by definition an amplifier.

Like many scientific discoveries the transistor was an unintentional discovery. Bell Telephone attempted to patent their discovery but it was deemed to be a natural phenomena, not an industrial design. Although primarily an amplifier, the most common use of a transistor is as a switch, enabling it, and its myriad associates on an integrated circuit, to respond to and generate digital information, that is, machine code, which is merely a series of on/off signals.

Transmission Control Protocol (TCP): Part of the TCP/IP stack. It functions on the transport layer (layer 4) of the OSI Model, establishing and verifying the data connection.

Transmitting: This word describes the process of sending data from one person to another, or from one computer to another, or from a remote peripheral, such as a telemetry device, to a computer. The verb is "to transmit the noun is "transmission".

Transmit network: A network that communicates with at least two other networks and transmits data among networks as well as among local nodes.

Transport layer: Layer 4 of the OSI Model, controlling delivery and verification of messages.

Tree administrator: In a tape tree, the person who designs the tree and administers the process, not necessarily the person who provides the seed (usually not, in fact).

trn: A threaded newsreader for UNIX based on rn.

Troff: A UNIX text processor that can produce output for typesetting equipment, superseded largely by TEX.

Trojan horse: An attack program, hidden inside a seemingly benign program, that enables the program's creator to gain access to the user's system.

Troll: *(v) 1.* To deliberately post egregiously false information to a newsgroup in hopes of tricking dense know-it-alls into correcting you; 2. From the fishing term, to explore information sources or communication methods on the Net, looking for something specific, as in the *New Yorker* cartoon in which a boss tells his employee: "I hear you've been trolling for babes on the Internet."

Trumpet newsreader Windows newsreader: software that works with NNTP, available by anonymous FTP from biochemistry.cwru.edu.

Trumpet for Windows: Windows Internet software featuring a newsreader and a mail program, available by anonymous FTP from biochemistry.cwru.edu.

Truth Table: A matrix of varying input events and the corresponding output events. Often used to show how a particular device will respond to particular inputs, that is, which outputs Will be generated by which inputs. Examples of truth tables can be found under the entries for AND Gate, Full Adder, Half Adder, NAND Gate, NOR Gate, OR Gate, XOR Gate.

TSR: Abbreviation for Terminate and Stay Resident, a phrase applied to many computer programs. TSR programs will run through to completion and then remain in RAM until the computer is turned off or reset, or a specific command is given to clear that particular part of RAM, this usually requires machine specific knowledge of the hardware and programming experience. TSRs sometimes suffer from memory clashes when two TSRs, written by two different programmers/software developers, may be directed to occupy the same portions of RAM, creating much confusion! See also Deadly Embrace, Kernel.

T3: A longdistance, digital, point-to-point communi-cations circuit, developed by AT&T, that transmits a signal at 44.746 Mbps, with up to 28 T1 channels (762 voice channels of 64 Kbps), running over a leased line, usually fiber-optic cable.

T2: A longdistance, digital, point-to-point communi-cations circuit, developed by AT&T, that transmits a signal at 6.3 Mbps, with up to four T1 channels (92 channels of 64 Kbps). T2 is used within telephone company networks, not commercially.

TTL: Abbreviation for Transistor-Transistor-Logic. This is a reference to a particular type of circuit technology that is used extensively in integrated circuits. An alternative technology is diode-transistor logic, however TTL is the most commonly used.

TTY: Abbreviation for teletypewriter. This is an outmoded name for the printer connected to a mainframe computer. Early TTY machines were often Telegraph/Telex machines and were not renowned for their sophistication.

The name TTY is sometimes used to describe a generic, unspecified printer. For example a word processing package may include a printer driver for a TTY. Such a driver would provide only very basic output.

Tunafish test: A series of posts in 1994 to a *.test newsgroup via the anon.penet.fi anonymous remailer service that may have compromised the identities of some of the remailer's users.

Turbo: Jargon used to indicate high processing speeds and/or slick operation. It is often used to describe specific brands of hardware and software.

TurboGopher: 1. A gopher client for the Macintosh, available via anonymous FTP from sumex-aim.stanford.edu; 2. An improved version of the original gopher software developed at the University of Minnesota.

Twisted-pair cable: Cable comprising four or more copper wires, twisted in pairs to reduce interference, usually one pair for sending, one for receiving. There are two types of twisted-pair cable: shielded twisted-pair (STP) and unshielded twisted-pair (UTP).

Tymnet: A global public data network, offering local dial-up access in one hundred countries, including access to some online services and Internet service providers.

Typeface: A style of lettering, often designed for a specific purpose, for example, readability in small sizes, for display purposes in large sizes, to attract the reader's attention, to create a particular mood or impression etc.

U

Undo: A feature of some software applications which allows the user to go back one step and revert to the data file, word processor document, spreadsheet etc., as it was before the last command. This is a very useful feature if a command is given in error or the outcome of a command is not as predicted.

Unerase: A feature of some utility software applications which enables previously 'erased' files to be recovered (erasing a file only removes the File Allocation Table entry, the data itself is not usually removed).

UN*X: A generic term for the various flavors and ports of UNIX, used also to refer to UNIX without including the TM notice erroneously thought to be required by AT&T.

Unbalanced line: A cable containing electrically unequal wires, such as a coaxial cable.

Uncompress: (v) To unsquish a compressed file.

Uncompression: A method of unsquishing a compressed file.

UnCover: A search service provided by CARL with access to over ten thousand journals.

Undelete: To restore a deleted file. This is not possible on UNIX systems.

Undernet: A network of IRC servers formed as an alternative to EFnet, the mainstream" IRC net. Undernet IRC servers always have domain names of the form *city. state*.undernet.org or *city.country*.undernet.org.

Undirected information: Inform-ation intended for the public at large, such as Usenet or mailing list Posts.

Unerase: A feature of some utility software applications which enables previously "erased" files to be recovered (erasing a file only removes the File Allocation Table entry, the data itself is not usually removed).

Unicode: A standard 16-bit character code (as compared with ASCII, which is a 7-bit character code) with 65,536 possible characters, as well as the ability to encode color and graphics. A possible eventual successor to ASCII.

Uniform resource locator (URL): A Web address. It consists of a protocol, a host name, a port (optional), a directory (optional), and a file name (optional). In the URL http://enterzone.berkeley. edu/ enterzone.html, the proto-col is HTTP, the host name is enterzone.berkeley.edu, and the file name is enterzone.html.

Uninterruptable Power Supply: A battery and/or generator supplemented power supply that is supposed to provide "no-break" conditions during a blackout. Batteries are used with static invertors to provide a standard AC 240v/50Hz supply during the immediate post-blackout period. The generator then takes over. An Uninterruptable Power Supply (abbreviation UPS) will often be used to guarantee power supply to large computer installations and those where shutdown would be unacceptable.

Universal Asynchronous Receiver/ Transmitter (UART): A device that combines the transmitting and receiving functions of asynchronous communications over a serial line.

Universal Time Coordinate (UTC): Greenwich mean time, used to synchronize computers on the Internet.

University of Maryland Info Database: A huge information resource intended to demonstrate the breadth of potential information on the Net. Telnet to info.umd.edu and log in as info.

UNIX: An operating system originally developed by American Telephone and Telegraph (AT&T) during the early 1970s. Several different versions are now supported by software developers, for example, IBM AIX, Microsoft Xenix etc. UNIX is widely used on mainframe computers and increasingly on PCs and workstations. It provides for multi-tasking and multiple users. See also Multi-tasking, Operating System.

UNIX box: A computer running the UNIX operating system.

Unix2dos: A program that converts UNIX text files to DOS format, by changing die line breaks.

UNIX weenie: 1. A programmer who has to use UNIX but would prefer not to: 2. Someone who admits to liking UNIX.

UNIX wizard: A helpful UNIX expert, such as those who answer questions in the comp.unix.wizards newsgroup.

Unmoderated: Said of lists and newsgroups whose posts are not vetted by a moderator.

Unread: (adj) Said of newsgroup articles that the user has not yet read or has marked as such. Unread articles will show up again the next time the user returns to the newsgroup.

Unselect articles: (v) To remove the selection tag from Usenet articles selected for reading.

Unshielded cable: Cable that's not protected from electromagnetic or radio-frequency interference by a foil shield.

Unshielded twisted-pair (UTP): A cable containing unshielded wire in twisted pairs.

Unsubscribe: 1. To remove one's name from a mailing list; 2. To remove the nəme of a newsgroup from the list of subscribed groups.

Untar: (v) To separate a tarred file into its component parts.

Up: (adj) Working, function-ing just fine, turned on.

Up-and-Running: Jargon for a computer that is functioning normally. Often used to describe a computer that has been out of action for a period of time but is now functioning normally.

Update: To change the contents of a data file in order to incorporate all of the latest amendments, deletions, changes, addi-tions etc.

Upgrade: 1) To modify hardware/software in order to eliminate bugs. 2) A new version of an existing software package or hardware. For example, "Upgrades of Z-Base are now available". Software is regularly upgraded as new aspects, requirements etc. are developed, and/or bugs are removed. Upgrades are usually sold at discount rates to users of previous versions.

Upload: To transfer a file over a modem from a desktop computer to a remote computer.

Urban legend: A story passed around and usually attributed to a *FOAF* (a friend of a friend), frequently (but not always) based on a kernel of falsehood. The newsgroup, alt.folklore. urban (and its less noisy cousin alt.folklore.suburban) is the home of UL debunkers.

U.S. Department of Defense (DoD): The original funder of ARPA and hence ARPAnet, the predecessor to the Internet.

Usenet: 1. From *User Network* and often written *USENET,* the collection of computers and networks that share news articles. Usenet is *not* the Internet (though it overlaps pretty well). It's sometimes called the world's largest electronic bulletin board. 2. The newsgroups in die traditional newsgroup hierarchies.

Usenet, Oracle: A cooperative project of mostly humorous questions and oracular responses. Anyone can submit questions or answers. To find out more about the Oracle, send mail to oracle@cs.indiana.edu with the word *help* in the Subject line, or read the rec.humor. oracle news-group.

User Datagram Protocol (UDP): A connectionless transport protocol in the TCP/IP suite. UDP is used for Simple Network Manage-ment Protocol, database lookups, and other functions instead of TCP, because it does not add overhead to the transmission.

User Friendly: A phrase used to describe computer software that is tolerant to mistakes and/or incomplete understanding of hardware/ software capabilities. User friendly packages usually give informative, polite messages when the user makes a mistake.

User Group: A society or club whose common interest is a hardware or software product, for example, MacIntosh Users Group, dBase Users Group.

Utility: A generic name for miscellaneous software applications and utilities. Ibis includes disk managers, operating system adjuncts, file retrieval and handling programs.

UUCP: From Unix to Unix Copy Program, a protocol and a program for copying files, news, and mail from one UNIX box to another during intermittent dial-up connections.

UUCPNET: An international store-and-forward network of UNIX machines (and others) that use the UUCP protocol to exchange mail and news, which is where Usenet originated.

uuencode: *(you-you-encode,* n) A UNIX program that converts binary files into an ASCII format suitable for inclusion in an e-mail message.

V

Vacuum Tube: An electronic device that uses a glass tube to house electronic circuitry, the workings of which are dependent on the vacuum within the tube. Vacuum tubes, also known as valves, were in widespread use until about the mid-1960s, when they were gradually replaced by solid state technology (transistors) which do not require a vacuum for their operation. Vacuum tube based computers required large amounts of space and cooling facilities and were heavy, and sometimes unwieldy, consumers of power.

Value Added Service: A term used in data communications which refers to resources or services added to a communications link above and beyond those normally offered by a common carrier. Value Added Services may be offered by the common carrier or by another organisation who is, in effect, a subcontractor to the common carrier.

Vapourware: A term used to describe hardware or software that is so long in arriving from the developer/manufacturer that no one believes it exists!

Variable: An entity defined in a computer program that is used to represent an item of data input by the user, any intermediate calculations and the end results.

VAX: A proprietary operating system developed by DEC (Digital Equipment Corporation) which is widely used on mini and small mainframe computers. The VAX operating system has an extensive command structure where most commands can be abbreviated to three letters, for example, dir can be entered instead of directory, mail instead of mail, edi instead of edit and so on.

VCR Backup: The use of a video cassette recorder to backup the contents of a hard disk. Many organisations use this method. A 90 minute video tape will hold about 100MB of data.

Vertical Redundancy Cheek: An error checking technique used in data communications in which the parity check character is applied to each row ofbits within a data block.

Video Card: The control interface for a monitor.

Video RAM: An area of RAM used exclusively by a computer monitor. Video RAM is updated as required by the CPU and in turn, Video RAM updates and refreshes the screen image. Direct access to Video RAM is usually only via assembly language programming.

Virtual Machine: A mainframe operating system philosophy that aims to give the user the impression that they have exclusive use of the computer. It is said that the mainframe terminal is virtually a sole user machine (computer).

Virtual Memory: An operating system technique that uses swapping techniques to increase the apparent size of actual memory. Machines operating under virtual operating systems are said to have a "virtual memory of ??MB". The virtual memory always being much greater than the actual (physical) memory.

Virus: A software program that affects the integrity of the operating system and/or data files. Virus programs have originated in several different countries, with the authors being unknown. Viruses are usually capable of reproducing themselves and can spread rapidly throughout an organisation's computer system. A virus may be introduced intentionally, for example, by a disgruntled employee, or unintentionally, for example, by taking infected disks from one computer to another. Fortunately "vaccine" software is now widely available and some measure of control can be achieved.

Visual Table of Contents: A chart which shows in graphical form the details of data flow within the organisation or within a specific computer program.

There is usually an increase in the amount of detail shown from the top of the chart to the bottom.

VLSI: Abbreviation for Very Large Scale Integration. This is a process used in the manufacture of integrated circuits 'which places hundreds of thousands of electronic circuits into one silicon chip.

Vnn: A series of standards developed by CCITT, for example, V.21 for 300 Baud data communications over telephone lines, V.22 1200 Baud, V.22bis (an extension of V.22, bis = Latin for twice) etc.

Voice Coil: A hard disk drive read/write head mechanism that provides fast access times, but is generally more expensive 1 than "conventional" (stepper) drives. Voice Coil technology uses a mechanism similar to that found in a loudspeaker.

Depending on the strength of the signal provided, the coil moves a fixed distance and is positioned over the required data storage track.

Given the lightness of the voice coil mechanism and its method of operation, access times are typically about 30ms, compared to 60-100ms on conventional mechanisms.

Voice Recognition: A comparatively new technology that enables computer hardware /software to recognise human speech.

Volatile Memory: This is a phrase used to describe a computer's primary memory (storage). The word volatile implies, usually correctly, that this memory will lose all its data once the power is turned off.

Volume: Any secondary storage medium, for example, a floppy disk, hard disk, CD-ROM etc. Each floppy disk, CD-ROM etc. is a volume and may be assigned a volume name or number.

Volume Table of Contents: A File allocation table for hard disks under Apple DOS (Disk Operating System).

VSAT: Abbreviation for Very Small Aperture Terminal, a microwave terminal with an aperture of approximately two metres. VSATs are often used for microwave transmission in remote localities, using satellites.

WAIS: Manager for Windows. Windows WAIS client software available via anonymous FTP from sunsite. unc.edu.

Wait State: The delay (wasted machine cycles) in processor activities which allow for the turnaround time from data request to data receipt, computers typically have zero, one or two wait states.

Wide Area Network: A computer network whose participants are separated by large distances. A typical Wide Area Network (abbreviation WAN) would cross state borders and have computers in Perth, Adelaide, Brisbane, Townsville and Sydney.

Wanna: Short for *wannafuck*, an unsolicited sexual inquiry, usually from a man to a woman (or someone with a possibly female name or username, especially someone who participates in sex-related newsgroups).

Warez: *(wares)* An old BBS term for pirated game software, still heard mostly in B1FFspeak.

Waflord: (v) To post someone else's large, ugly, or stupid sig block to the alt.fan.warlord newsgroup and then cut it down to size (from the username of a newbie with a BUAG medieval sword in his sig).

Warm boot: (v) To reboot a computer without turning it off.

Warm Link: A software link between two data files. A, one file is updated the other is also (automatically) updated.

Warnier-Orr Chart: A chart that shows generalised processes on one side (usually the left side) and progressively more detail towards the right. The Warnier-Crr Chart was devised by Jean-Dominique Warnier and Ken Orr during the 1970s. This type of chart is sometimes used in program design to show the dependency of one particular process or data item on another.

Washington University Services: A gateway to many IInternet services, libraries, and other information resources. To use it, telnet to wugate.wustl.edu and log in as services.

Waste bandwidth: (v) To misuse system resources (even having too long a sig block is sometimes enough to bring out accusations of wasting bandwidth).

Watch Point: A step inserted into a program for debugging purposes. Watch Points usually display the contents of a particular memory location (variable).

Weather: There are many weather information servers on the Internet. For weather information, telnet to madlab.sprl.umich.edu, port 3000; or wind. atmos.uah.edu, port 3000.

Web: The most commonly used name for the World *Wide Web,* an interlinked collection of hypertext documents Web pages) residing on Web servers and other documents, menus, and databases, available via URLs (uniform resource locators). Web documents are marked for formatting and linking with HTML (hypertext markup language), and Web servers use HTTP (hypertext transport protocol) to deliver Web pages.

The Web was invented as an online documentation resource by physicists at the CERN European Particle Physics Laboratory in Switzerland.

Web address: A URL, consisting of a protocol, a host name, a path, and a file name. In the address of my home page, http://enterzone.berkeleyedu/homics/xian.html, the protocol is HTTP, the host name is enterzone.berkeley.edu, the path is /homies/and the file name is xian.html.

Web browser: Client software for the World Wide Web, such as www, lynx, Mosaic, or Netscape. A Web browser displays HTML and other documents, and allows the user to follow hypertext links.

Web page: An HTML document on the World Wide Web, usually containing hypertext links to other documents on the Web, often on other Web servers entirely.

Web server: An application that stores Web pages and associated files, databases, and scripts, and serves up the pages to Web browsers, using HTTP.

Weenie: 1. A luser,. 2. A hacker deeply involved in a particular operating system (such as a UNIX weenie).

Wetware: Also *liveware,* slang for human beings, seen as part of a greater computer system including software and hardware.

Whatis: An archie command that looks for key words in a software-description database containing file names and associated descriptions, used to find key words to search for.

Wheel: (n) A privileged user, someone with unrestricted access to some particular system resource.

Whitehouse.gov: The domain of the executive branch of the U.S. government.

White Noise: Any interference on a communications line that is of many indeterminate frequencies, hence the name, white noise.

White pages: Informal name for databases of Internet e-mail addresses or other information. For example, telnet to wp.psi.net and log in as *fred.*

White Space Character: A character that does not necessarily appear on-screen, for example, a space, tab, line return etc. Many word processors provide the option of viewing or not viewing these characters.

Whois: One of many online databases of Internet e-mail addresses and other identifying information about users, admins, domains, and so on: 2. The UNIX command that draws on the, resource.

Wild Card: A character inserted into an operating system command that is interpreted as having several meanings. For example the MS-DOS command "Erase *.doc" will erase all files with the file extension doc. In another example the VAX command "Purge Prog26*" will delete all but the most up-to-date, versions of Prog26 files. Wild cards are useful productivity tools but can, create havoc if an erroneous command is given.

WIMP: (adj) From *Window Icon, Menu, Pointing device,* said of a graphical user interface such as Macintosh. Windows, or X.

Winchester Disk: A particular type of hard disk technology which uses a high density of data storage tracks and a very low flying read/write head ' requiring a closely controlled operating environment. Winchester technology was developed by IBM and first introduced in 1973.

Window: This is part of the on-screen display on a monitor. The display may use only one window, occupying most of the available space.

Windows: A proprietary adjunct to the MS-DOS operating system. Windows was developed by Microsoft and provides enhanced file handling features and the ability to load more than one program at once.

Windows 95: The version of Windows. It is rumored to include TCP/IP support as well as direct access to Microsoft Network, which itself will include full access to the Internet.

Windows NT: A 32-bit operating system based on the Windows operating environment with built-in networking capabilities and no remaining traces of DOS.

Windows socket: The conventional method of configuring the Windows operating environment, for TCP/IP networking.

Windows for Workgroups: A version of Windows with built-in peer-to-peer networking capabilities.

Windoze: A derogatory term for Windows, referring to its legendary slowness.

Winqvt/Net: Combined mail, news, telnet, FTP for Windows.

Winsock: A type of Windows application that sets up a socket and works with TCP/IP protocols to establish an Internet connection.

WinVN: A newsreader for Windows based on the UNIX vn newsreader that communicates with Network News Transfer Protocol-based news servers, available via anonymous FTP from titan.ksc.nasa.gov.

WinWAIS: A Windows WAIS client program, available via anonymous FTP from ridgisd.er.usgs.gov.

WinWeb: A Web browser for Windows, created by EINET, and available via anonymous FTP from ftp.einet.net in the /einet/pc/winweb directory.

Wizard: Someone who really understands how a piece of hardware or software works and is willing to help newbies; 2. By extension, any expert, as in the alt.sex.wizards newsgroup.

Word: The basic storage unit of a computer, typically one word occupies two or more bytes of memory.

Word Processor: A software package that is primarily concerned with the entry, manipulation and formatting of text.

Word Wrap: A feature of most word processors which ensures that a word that will not fit at the end of a line of text will automatically be placed at the start of the next (new) line.

Workaround: A temporary patch for a bug that avoids but does not fix the underlying problem.

Workgroup: A group of users, often on a LAN, working on the same project.

Working Directory: The directory currently being used for data transfers.

Workstation: This is essentially a PC (micro-computer), often in a network environment. Increasingly workstations are becoming synonymous with superior processing capabilities, however many workstations are fairly ordinary machines. A diskless workstation does not have floppy disk drives, data storage is provided by a centralised hard disk. This provides management control over data storage as it reduces the likelihood of data theft, the introduction of computer virus, and of employees running their own software.

World: The default distribution choice for newsgroup posts. Post distribution can also be limited to geographical areas (by their two-letter abbreviations) or to local.

World Wide Web: Also called the Web, WWW, W3, and w^3, an interlinked collection of hypertext documents (Web pages) residing on Web servers and other documents, menus, and databases, available via URLs (uniform resource locators).

The Web was invented as an online documentation resource by physicists at the CERN European Particle Physics Laboratory in Switzerland.

Worm: A program that duplicates itself repeatedly, potentially worming its way through an entire network.

WORM Drive: A Write-Once-Read-Many times optical disk drive which can be of varying size and which is an increasingly important form of secondary memory. A 30Omm diameter disk has a storage capacity of about 6GB, 5.25" (135mm) disks hold about 800MB.

WPO: Abbreviation for Word Processor Operator, a person who is trained to use a word processor.

:wq The save *and quit* command in vi, often seen at the end of newbies' posts when they fail to switch back from insert mode to edit mode before typing the command.

Write: The process of entering data into primary memory or secondary memory.

Write Protection: A technique used to prevent accidental or intentional alteration/deletion of important data and/or programs, for example, the operating system.

X

Xerox PARC: Xerox's legendary Palo Alto Research Center, where the modem GUI was invented, not to metion laser printers and LANs.

X.500: A CCITT and standard for electronic using a distributed database of X.400 information, including usernames, postal addresses, telephone numbers, fax numbers, and so on.

X.400: A CCITT and ISO standard for international e-mail handling.

XGopher: X Window gopher client ware, available via anonymous FTP from boom box.micro.umn.edu.

Xibo: The evil anti-Kibo. This unfortunate devil has many fewer adherents than his nemesis.

XLibrary for the Macintosh Macintosh: software for designing SLIP front ends to network services, via anonymous FTP from sumexaim. stanford.edu.

Xmodem: A file-transfer protocol sup ported by just about every program.

Xmodem-CRC: An extension of Xmodern using more stringent errorchecking.

XON/XOFF: A form of flow control, using ASCII characters 17 and 19 to control the flow of data over an asychronous connection, usually one of the choices for configuring a modern to connect to a dial-up service.

XOR: [Boolean operator] *Exclusive or. A* text search with XOR between two words matches any documents containing one word or the other, but not both.

Y

YACC: Acronym for yet another complier. A widely used complier provided as a part of the Unix operating system.

Year: A dBASE function that returns a number being the year of its date argument.

Yoke: A pair of group of read-write head that are fastened together and move as a unit over two or more adjacent tracks on magnetic tape or disk.

Y-punch: Punch in the top most or 12th row of punched card.

Z

Zen and the Art *of* the Internet: Brendan Kehoe's excellent Internet primer, available as a paper book from Prentice Hall and online from many FTP and gopher sites (try an archie or Veronica search), including via anonymous FTP from ftp.cs.widener. edu in the directory pub/zen.

Zine: Also zine, a fanzine or other underground publication, possibly produced on company time or using office equipment.

Zip: (v) To compress a file with pkzip or another program.

Zip: A file extension indicating that the file has been compressed with the programs pkzip, zip, or WinZip.

Zip codes: U.S. postal zip codes as of 1991 can be found via anonymous FTP from oes.orst.edu in the /pub/almanac/misc directory with the file name zipcode.txt.Z.

Zmodem: A batch filetransfer protocol supported by some communications programs.

Zone: (n) A logical (as opposed to physical) group of users on a LAN, such as thin an AppleTalk network, within a larger group of interconnected networks.

